A HIGHER CALLING

The Dan Miller Story

A HIGHER CALLING

The Dan Miller Story

DAN MILLER

REDEMPTION
PRESS

Published by Redemption Press, PO Box 427, Enumclaw, WA 98022

Toll Free (844) 2REDEEM (273-3336)

Redemption Press is honored to present this title in partnership with the author. The views expressed or implied in this work are those of the author. Redemption Press provides our imprint seal representing design excellence, creative content, and high quality production.

All Scripture is taken from the New American Standard Bible, © Copyright 1960, 1962, 1963, 1968, 1971, 1973, 1975, 1977 by The Lockman Foundation. Used by permission.

ISBN 13: 978-1-68314-345-1 (Paperback)
978-1-68314-348-2 (Hard Cover)
978-1-68314-346-8 (ePub)
978-1-68314-347-5 (Mobi)

Library of Congress Catalog Card Number: 2017956070

Dedication

HOW DOES ONE DEDICATE THEIR life's story to only one or a few people who have been influential in their life?

In my case, dedicating this story to my wife Priscilla, my daughter Jessica, my son Jim, my granddaughter Hope, and grandson Aidan, is easy.

But so many people over the years have had a positive influence on my life.

I especially am grateful to the men and women of Mercer Island Covenant Church. Even though they had never met me and knew very little about me, they prayed for me over ten years because I was the nephew of one of their members, my aunt Margaret. They didn't give up on me even though, as my aunt said to me one day, "The more we prayed, the worse you got."

So, I dedicate this book to the many people who throughout my Christian walk with God, have loved me, challenged me, rebuked me, cared for me, mentored me, and are my friends.

Thank you; from the bottom of my heart, thank you.

Acknowledgments

FOR MANY YEARS, AS EVENTS and experiences have come to mind, I have written them down and filed them away with the thought that someday I might put them together in story form for my children and grandchildren. What started out to be an "interesting project," has turned into a major undertaking.

Over the years, as people have gotten to know me and have heard my testimony or bits and pieces of my life story, they have encouraged me to publish my story for others to read.

I had put this idea off for many years because I'm, for the most part, a behind-the-scenes kind of guy.

With the encouragement of my wife Priscilla, I hired Redemption Press to give me some professional guidance. We both felt that if I was going to put my story in a form that others will read, then I should do it right. I am deeply grateful for my editor, Inger. She helped this completely inexperienced writer, and I'm taking liberties calling myself a writer, and patiently helped me put my story in the form you see today.

I hope my life story will help you and others to not make the mistakes I made and to be encouraged by the way the Lord has transformed my life.

Each of you has your own story to tell.

Contents

Preface

I'M IN MY SEAT ON a Boeing 707 on the tarmac of San Francisco International Airport, trying to look as cool as a twenty-one-year-old guy should look on his way to the adventure of a lifetime.

How do I work these seatbelts? We didn't have seatbelts in our cars. *How did I ever survive without seatbelts riding in the back of a pickup and tearing down a mountain logging road at fifty to sixty miles per hour?*

Ah there, the seatbelt clicks into place. *I'm ready to roll. This country boy's going places.*

As the engine's roar seems to go right through me and the plane lifts off the ground, I grip the armrests and give my best friend John a lopsided "we-can-do-this" grin. I don't want to admit it, but I'm feeling both scared and excited at the same time.

I was on my way to helicopter school, and I knew my life would never be the same. But I didn't know then I would log over 2,700 hours in a helicopter as a pilot and fly as a passenger over 100,000 miles a year commercially in the corporate world.

I didn't know that I'd go through a dark time when gambling had its grip on me, and I was running with the wrong people. Those dark years would cause great pain and anguish to everyone I loved and cared about.

If not for a life-changing evening on December 7, 1976, I have no doubt that I would be either dead or in prison today.

Let me tell you my story.

ONE

Skinny Country Boy

SUMMER NIGHTS IN THE NORTHERN California college town of Chico often found me sleeping under the stars. My friends, David Serpa, Bunkey "Bubba" Taylor, and David Jones and I would swat mosquitoes and tell each other scary stories or recount some dangerous or exciting adventure we had gone on since the last time we were together. During the summer, that was just about every week.

Summers were hot and steamy in the northern part of the Sacramento Valley with temperatures averaging between 95 and 105 degrees during the day.

We had great times looking up at the Milky Way on moonless nights pondering great cosmic questions such as, "Where does it all end?" and "If there is an end, what is the end made of?"

"Hey guys," Bubba asked, "What do you think's holding everything together?"

Just eleven- and twelve-year-old boys, we'd lie under the stars in one or the other's backyard and wonder about the universe and our place in it.

Life was good growing up in Chico where I was born. Looking back, I'd say I had just about the perfect boy's life growing up. A naturally skinny kid, I seemed to be stronger than many of my friends. Maybe it was because I was always making forts in the woods near where we lived, climbing trees and exploring areas I probably should have stayed out of.

"Danny, put some clothes on!" my mother would holler at me as I dashed out for another summer adventure, barefoot and often without a shirt.

Bidwell Park was tailor-made for the adventures my gang of friends and I went on. It's a wooded park that stretches over five miles with a stream running through it. Filled with hundreds of oak trees, it had, what was at the time, the largest oak tree in the world. In 1938, part of the original *Robin Hood* movie with Errol Flynn was filmed in Bidwell Park.

There was no lack of friends to go off exploring places with. Or I'd just roam around on my own to find areas I had not been to before. Sometimes I'd sit for hours next to a small stream in a meadow just observing what was around me.

I was one of those rambunctious kids who'd come home dirty and often scratched and bruised. Mom and Dad seemed to have very little control over my reckless behavior, or maybe they just couldn't catch me. New shirts and pants would need mending and patching after just a few weeks of use.

Mom told someone once, "I pray Danny will live to see his eighteenth birthday."

We didn't have much money in those days, but I had wonderful, loving, and caring parents.

Dad taught me how to fix and make all kinds of things, how to pan for gold, fish, hunt, shoot pistols, rifles and shotguns, use a hunting knife, and survive in the wilderness. He also taught me honesty, good money management, respecting others, and not taking credit for things others had done.

Mom was a loving and creative mother who taught me how to be loving, caring, and respectful of others. She also taught me how to cook, wash and iron my own clothes, and sew on buttons. She wanted to prepare me for college and life in general.

✈ TWO ✈

Playing in Paradise

DAD WAS HOME ON LEAVE from the US Marine Corps when I was born in October of 1944. A few weeks later, he was shipped overseas with his battalion and didn't see me again until I was two and a half years old. To earn extra money while he was overseas, Mom danced as a ballerina in the San Francisco Ballet. Dad received an honorable discharge from the Marines in 1945.

In 1948, Mom and Dad went from San Francisco to Paradise, California and moved in with Mom's Aunt Dodie and Uncle Dude.

In 1949, they purchased a piece of property just outside the town of Paradise, a town of about 2,000 people located in the foothills about twenty miles from Chico. Dad and his older sister's husband, George, built our house, a two-bedroom rambler with a small one-car garage.

My sister Julie, who is four years younger than me, and I shared one of the bedrooms. I slept on the top of a bunk bed, and Julie slept in a crib.

Dad brought home a brown mongrel puppy for me that I named Ginger. Ginger and I hit it off right away, and we did everything together. Mom used to say, "I seldom worry about where Danny is. All I have to do is call Ginger, and he'll be right behind." He was my best friend while we lived in Paradise as there weren't any kids my age who lived near us.

Ginger loved to chase squirrels and play in the water with me. I'd tie a rope around his neck—he had grown up to be a big dog by then—and tie the other end to the handle of my Red Flyer wagon so he could pull me around our yard. That probably wasn't as much fun for him as it was for me.

On summer days, I'd grab my Red Flyer, call Ginger, and head down our driveway to explore the "dangerous wilderness" surrounding our home. Parents didn't seem to worry much in those days about a five-year-old playing alone in the woods or wandering around the neighborhood—after all, I was almost six.

During our regular adventures into the wilderness, Ginger would chase squirrels and dig in the dirt while I remained on constant alert for bandits and wild tigers, a game Ginger and I loved to play. Our adventures in the "wilderness" were all within a few of blocks of our home, of course.

Ginger and I often visited an old man who lived about a quarter of a mile from our house who kept two "gigantic" jackasses in a corral. On an occasion, without my parents knowing, he would let me ride one of them around the corral. Ginger didn't approve of this activity at all, and he'd indicate his disapproval by his constant barking.

We lived at the end of a long dirt road outside of town that Dad had named "Fern Lane." Dad grew all kinds of ferns to earn extra money in a large greenhouse he had built in the back of our house.

I liked following him around the yard, watching all the things he did and helping him whenever he "needed" my help, which seemed to be quite often.

I had watched him put gas in our car from time to time. One day, as my parents were sitting on the front porch enjoying the warm afternoon and sipping some cool drink, I decided to help Dad out. As my parents thought their son was playing innocently in the yard, I took the gas cap off the car and poured muddy water into the gas tank.

They didn't realize what their wonderful son was doing until they saw my muddy hands and clothes as I came from around the car towards them. I don't remember getting into trouble other than receiving some specific instructions about what makes a car run, and it wasn't on water!

Dad had to remove the gas tank and completely flush and clean the tank before reinstalling it on the car. Cars were a lot easier to work on in those days. At least that's what I rationalize to make me feel a little better about what I did.

Christmas was always an exciting time for me. Julie and I didn't get many gifts, but there always seemed to be at least one gift I had asked for. My gifts also included the usual socks, underwear and something knitted by an aunt. It wasn't the gifts that made Christmas fun, instead it was the unintentional tradition Dad and Uncle Ken started when I was four or five years old.

We always celebrated Christmas at Aunt Jess's and Uncle Ken's house, not real relatives, but neighbors of Mom and her Aunt Dodie. Aunt Jess helped take care of me from time to time while Dad was away overseas during WW II. (A very special person in my life, she accepted Jesus as her Savior and Lord while in her 90s and died at 102.)

One Christmas, Dad gave Uncle Ken a stick-on tinted windshield visor to reduce the glare of the sun in his car as cars didn't come standard with tinted windshields in those days. The green visor came folded up in a box. To install it, you would unfold and smooth out the visor on an ironing board, put a towel over the visor and heat it with a hot clothes iron. Then quickly, while it was still warm, place it inside and on top of the front windshield of the car.

When Uncle Ken opened Dad's gift, everyone could see it wasn't received with much enthusiasm.

The following Christmas, we were opening our presents when Dad burst out laughing. We all turned to see what was so funny and there he was holding the tinted windshield visor in the same unopened box he had given Uncle Ken the year before. Uncle Ken, normally a serious person, was grinning from ear to ear.

This exchange went on for years; each year, whoever had received the visor the previous year, would try to disguise it by wrapping it up in some very creative way. One Christmas, Dad put it in about six other boxes, each one inside the other.

Twelve or thirteen years after this tradition had begun, the last of the gifts had been opened, and everyone waited with great anticipation for the visor to be opened, but it never came. Dad thought Ken had received the visor last and Ken thought Dad had it last. None of us could remember who had ended up with it the previous Christmas. Dad was convinced Ken had enough of this "tradition" and had thrown it away. Christmas would never be the same.

My parents' best friends from high school and junior college, Richard and Jeannie, lived near us in Paradise. Sometimes when I went over to their house, I would get to milk their cow and from time to time, ride one of their Appaloosa horses. We kids always rode bareback and would ride as fast as we could down the rows of the apple orchard near their house. The trick was to keep from getting hit in the face or knocked off the horse from one of the outstretched branches.

In high school, I'd occasionally get to ride one of my farmer friend's horses, always bareback of course. Many years in the future, I went riding with a friend of mine in the foothills of the Sierra Mountains. The horse I rode had a saddle and that made me feel uncomfortable because I couldn't feel the horse under me.

THREE

A Crystal Cave and Purple Bruises

WHEN I WAS SEVEN AND Julie three, we moved to Quincy, located in the Sierra Mountains at an elevation of 3,400 feet. Summers in Quincy were sunny and warm; winters, however, were cold and windy with lots of snow.

The fall of 1952 was exciting for me because I was to begin third grade in the largest elementary school in town, come to think of it, the only elementary school in town. As I was walking home from school one afternoon, my teacher began walking beside me. I wondered *Where is she going?* Then I discovered she lived in the house next to ours. I always had the unsettling feeling that my teacher was constantly looking out her window, checking to see if I was doing my homework.

Dad worked for the Pacific Gas & Electric Company. Mom loved being a housewife as well as belonging to various quilting, painting and other groups.

One day, one of the kids in my class asked, "Where did you get *that* shirt?" Another one asked, "Don't you have a pair of jeans?"

When I told them, "My mother makes my clothes," they laughed.

At home I told my parents what happened and, reluctantly, they got me some store-bought clothes. I'm sure this was hard for my mother because she was an excellent seamstress.

My friends and I would often harass each other into doing some foolish stunt, not ever considering the consequences of our actions. I guess it's a boy thing to do, and I seemed to take more chances than most.

As several of us were exploring the hills behind where I lived one day, we discovered a hole hidden among some bushes on the side of the hill. Tommy, the youngest of our gang, didn't want to go near the bushes because he was afraid of snakes.

I said, "Tommy, there aren't any snakes around here. It's too cold for snakes to live up here." That wasn't entirely true, but it sounded good. After much prodding and harassing, we convinced him that he was the only one who could fit into the opening because he was smaller than the rest of us. When Tommy finally ventured in, with a little encouragement (help) from the rest of us, he discovered a small cave full of clear rock crystals. Several of these crystals were eight to ten inches in length. We each dug out several of the crystals and proudly took them home. I'm not sure what happened to mine, they probably got lost in one of our many moves over the years.

As I was playing in our neighbor's vacant lot one afternoon, I discovered a long steel cable lying in the tall grass. The cable had a loop in it with a steel clamp holding the loop together. I thought this would be a great way to get up into the large tree in our front yard as I couldn't reach any of the branches. The consequences of this innovative idea seemed to elude me at the time.

I dragged the cable into the yard and proceeded to throw the loop end up and over the limb of the tree. I put one foot in the loop, and pulling on the other end of the cable, began to winch myself up to the tree limb above. About two feet above the ground, my foot slipped out of the loop causing the loop and cable to fly up and over the limb and crash down on my head, knocking me out cold.

As this was taking place, a linen delivery truck was coming down our street, and the driver witnessed the entire event. I woke up on our living room couch with a bloody towel on my head and Mom and the delivery truck driver standing over me. Mom took me to the doctor, but I don't remember him doing anything other than bandaging my head. Maybe that's why I have a slightly pointed head.

Several of us were playing in the front yard of a friend's house when one of the neighbor kids who was a couple of years older than the rest of us, whom we didn't like, came into the yard and demanded we let him play the game we were playing. This really made me mad because he didn't even ask. Of course, I would have said no if he had asked. The next thing I knew the two of us were fighting. He got in a lucky punch and hit me hard on my shoulder, which really hurt.

As I was picking myself off the ground, Mom drove by, stopped, and said, "Danny, get in the car right now." It seems I had forgotten I was supposed to have been home some fifteen minutes earlier because she needed to pick my sister up at her friend's house.

I didn't tell her about my hurting shoulder because then I would have had to tell her how it had happened. For some reason, Mom didn't approve of my fighting. I guess she didn't understand that boys' fighting now and then is just part of their initiation into manhood.

By the time we got home, the pain in my shoulder was unbearable. Reluctantly, I told her what had happened. My shoulder hurt so bad that I couldn't raise my arm above my head to take my shirt off. Mom had to cut my shirt off with a pair of scissors.

Mom gasped when she saw my shoulder. The entire area around my shoulder was badly swollen and black and blue down into my chest. She let me know how upset she was that I hadn't told her about my injury. "Don't you realize that some of your injuries could be internal?" she said. When Mom and Dad took me to the doctor, x-rays revealed I had a broken collarbone. This was my first broken bone of what would turn out to be many in the years to come.

That night Mom gave me a stern lecture, also one of many lectures I would receive in the future about how to treat others and that fighting was not what good boys did. (Actually, Mom's lectures were more like soft-spoken encouragements not to do what I had done than stern warnings.)

Dad didn't say anything, he just smiled at me. I would like to think he was proud of me for protecting my friends. I think he also got a lecture after I went to bed.

I lifted my shirt and showed anyone who was interested in seeing my black and blue body. All the guys thought my injuries looked "cool." I don't remember the girls I displayed my injuries to being all that impressed.

Our family often enjoyed having trout for dinner. When Mom wanted to have trout for dinner that night, I got out our fishing poles, dug some worms, and anxiously waited for Dad to get home from work. As soon as he got home and changed his clothes, we drove about a half a mile north of town to a narrow but deep stream that ran through a large meadow. The meadow was full of tall, dark green, almost purple grass, surrounded by pine tree forests.

We talked about how many fish each of us wanted to eat, and within fifteen minutes or less of arriving at the stream, we had caught what we needed.

I loved to ride my bicycle to that meadow. For what seemed to me like hours, I would lie in the grass taking in the sounds and smells around me. The water of the stream was fed by springs and snow run-off so the water was ice cold and sweet to drink.

⟜ FOUR ⟜

Scars

MOM AND DAD BOUGHT A house in a new housing development just north of Chico when I was nine years old. The house was a small two-bedroom rambler with a one-car garage and a large back yard with four full-grown almond trees. Within a year, Dad converted our garage into a bedroom for me and built a carport next to my bedroom.

Summers were filled with fun and adventures. My friends, David Serpa, David Jones and Bunkey "Bubba" Taylor and I would ride our bikes everywhere. Our family, as well as most families we knew, had only one car, so if I wanted to go somewhere, I either walked or rode my bike.

David Serpa loved to roller skate at the local roller rink. In high school he entered and won many skating pairs competitions.

David Jones was the brains of our small group. He was constantly telling us why we should or shouldn't do whatever we were doing. Why he hung out with the rest of us was a mystery. I don't ever remember David getting dirty.

Bubba's parents were from the South somewhere. I loved the way his mother spoke and the way she'd greet us with a big smile and a plate of cookies. Bubba was bigger than the rest of us and always seemed to be in some kind of trouble—well, more than me, anyway.

During the summer of 1954, on one of our many excursions around the area, David, Bubba, and I found a stream about two miles from our house that had a deep, wide pool in it. A tall oak tree leaned over the water with a long rope tied around a big branch that reached out eight or ten feet over the stream. It was about eight feet from the water to the top of the bank where the tree was. The ground sloped gradually upwards and away from the stream and there was a trail that ran about thirty feet behind the stream bank.

We got on our bikes as far back from the bank as possible, then rode as fast as we could down the slope with the idea of catching hold of the rope as we went flying off the bank into the air. Our bikes flew out of the way as we fell into the water below. We then dove down to the bottom of the pool to retrieve our bikes. The hard part was hauling the bike back up the bank to do it all again.

Several of us got very good at grabbing the rope as our bikes flew out from under us. To make things interesting, we challenged each other to not only grab the rope, but keep hold on our bikes with our legs as we swung back and forth over the water. When we let go of the rope, we'd then fall into the water sitting on our bikes. We thought this was very smart because we didn't have to dive down to the bottom of the pool to retrieve our bikes.

Doing stunts like this was probably one of the reasons why we were constantly repairing our bikes and coming home with cuts and bruises. We were always more than willing to display our injuries to any girl in our neighborhood who would listen to the accounts of our daring feats of bravery. I don't remember any of the girls I knew being that interested to hear about my adventures.

It seemed like I lived in the water during those long hot summer days. I loved the heat and would play outside when everyone else was in the house or under a tree trying to keep cool. Very few people had air conditioning in those days, but some of our neighbors had swamp coolers on top of their houses. They didn't seem to reduce the heat much but did create humidity.

One day during the summer of 1955, I was playing with some of the neighbor kids in Jack's front yard. Jack was a couple of years younger than I. While we were playing, his older brother came out carrying one of those toy bows that come with arrows with suction cups. But instead of play arrows, he had inserted one of his dad's flat bladed hunting arrows into the bow. He was laughing and pointing the arrow at us boys.

When he pointed it at me, I told him, "Stop it!" Whether intentionally or by accident, he let the arrow go. The arrow had enough force to fly at me and the point of the arrow stuck in my chin.

I pulled the arrow out and blood began streaming down my chin.

Neighbor kids began yelling, screaming, and crying. With all the commotion going on, parents came running out of their houses, probably thinking that one of us kids had been killed.

One of the kids ran to my house and got my mom. I have no idea what that kid told my mom, but she came running into the yard and said, "Danny, what did you do?" She didn't say, "What happened?" but assumed I was the one who had done something wrong, probably a natural reaction from many of my past exploits as I was constantly getting into mischief of one kind or another.

She saw the hunting arrow on the ground and my chin bleeding. Then the kids started yelling, "Jack's brother did it! Jack's brother did it!"

I stood there in shock as my sweet, gentle, always calm and smiling mother began yelling at Jack's brother and his mother who had come out to see what all the commotion was about. "You could have put Danny's eye out! What were you thinking?" That was the first and only time I can remember my mother getting verbally angry at anyone. You can still see the scar that arrow left in my chin.

During the summer of 1956, I was eleven. With sixth grade behind me, I was headed for seventh grade in the new junior-high school in town. We had been in a small, crowded elementary school where one of my classes was held in the hallway because there wasn't a classroom available.

One day I looked up in the tree that was in our front yard to find that a beehive had formed on one of the branches during the night. Finding a long stick, I proceeded to hit the hive thinking I would chase them away from our house and protect my family from getting stung. For some reason, the bees didn't appreciate the fact that I was destroying their home. The next thing I knew, I was surrounded by a swarm of angry bees. I ran into our back yard, grabbed a sprinkler that was running and put it on top of my head, as I swatted the bees off me. By the time they were finished with me, I had a couple of dozen bee stings all over my body since I seldom wore a shirt in the summer.

Mom heard me yelling while this was going on, but by the time she came to my rescue, it was over. She didn't realize I was in trouble at first because I was always running around the yard yelling and making all kinds of noise while playing.

The next day, we called a beekeeper and he took the hive away. I didn't have any swelling from the stings and seemed to be immune to bee or mosquito venom in the future.

David Serpa lived directly across the street from me, and we were always doing something together, especially fishing, our favorite.

About three miles from our homes was a swimming hole called the Five Mile Dam. The actual dam was only ten or fifteen feet high and had been given its name as it was about five miles from town. The dam made a great deep swimming area behind it where we would spend hours swimming and playing games in the water.

North of the dam was our favorite fishing area, an area full of deep potholes from five to ten feet in diameter with the water anywhere from eight to ten feet below the top of the bank.

Water ran underground connecting many of these holes and they were full of trout. David and I would stand at the edge of a hole and fish. If one of us had slipped and fallen into one of those holes, we would never have gotten out before help could arrive.

David's father was a county sheriff who raced stock cars at the county fairgrounds on weekends. I would often get to go with David and his dad to the races as his dad got us passes that allowed the two of us to wander around the pit area.

Mom didn't like me going with them because I always came home covered with dirt. She obviously didn't understand that part of a boy growing up was to regularly experience the feel of mud and dirt on one's face and clothes, or maybe she was just tired of washing the same clothes over and over again.

In 1955, the new and fantastic theme park, Disneyland, opened to the public in Anaheim, California. Newspapers reported the rides and events to be "the best in the world."

Mom and Dad began saving their money to take us. In the summer of 1957, the four of us drove from Chico to Anaheim, about a five-hundred-mile drive. Without air conditioning, the drive was long and hot with the temperatures around ninety to one hundred degrees, and the speed limit was fifty-five m.p.h.

At Disneyland, I was in awe of all the fantastic rides and mechanical animals and people. Today they might not seem quite as exciting to kids of the same age, but back then there was nothing that could compare to the size and technology of this theme park. My friends were very envious of me because I was the first one on our block to go to Disneyland.

While we were there, we took a side trip about forty miles south of Anaheim to visit Dad's older brother, Uncle Fred, and his wife Eva.

Uncle Fred was an aeronautical engineer working on some secret project that had something to do with rockets destined for outer space. At the time, this sounded really farfetched to me. He died of a massive heart attack while in his early sixties.

Dad and I often hiked down into some remote canyon to pan for gold. I think he taught me how to use a sluice box and a gold pan before he taught me how to ride a bike. This activity often resulted in our confronting a rattlesnake or two. It was hard, rough, dirty work but very rewarding when we saw the gold at the bottom of the pan glimmering in the sun against the black sand. We found gold on many of our trips; however, we never did find the mother lode.

Camping was always part of our summer activities as a family. We traveled to places like Banff in Alberta, Canada, Montana, Utah, Nevada, Arizona, and to parks all over California. Mom and Dad would often let us take a friend on many of our camping trips. Dad was a great camp cook as well as enjoying barbequing at home.

Other summer days my friends and I often played basketball at our school. One day in one of our more competitive games, I got hit hard in the nose by someone's elbow. My nose was broken and leaned to one side with blood gushing out onto my clothes and the ground. By the time I got home, I had a black eye and my nose was badly swollen.

It was a Saturday so Dad was home. We didn't have health insurance back then, so my dad took his two little fingers, shoved them up into my nostrils and proceeded to straighten my nose. He said, "Don't worry, it's only cartilage that's broken, it will grow back." I don't know where he learned that technique. He did a pretty good job; today you can barely tell my nose was ever broken.

From time to time, I rode my bike two miles into town to the *Enterprise Record*, our local newspaper. The paper would sell me ten newspapers for five cents each. I then walked up and down the streets of town and sold those newspapers for ten cents each, the selling price of the newspaper. A profit of fifty cents might not seem like much, but back then for five cents I could buy a bottle of pop or a candy bar, and for twenty-five cents, get into one of the three local movie houses in town.

I also earned twenty-five cents each week for mowing our front and back lawns with a push lawn mower.

While living in Chico, Mom and Dad helped form a new Congregational church where they were charter members. They enrolled me in a confirmation class, but to this day I don't remember anything about that class or any of the time spent in Sunday school. Why I have no memory of church or Sunday school during those years is baffling to me. It was most likely because while the teacher was talking, I was looking out the window dreaming of some fun adventure I was hoping to go on.

FIVE

In the Great Outdoors

DAD'S COMPANY TRANSFERRED HIM TO Willows, California the summer of 1957. Willows is located about thirty-six miles west of Chico and at the time, had a population of about 4,600 people. The town was surrounded by thousands of acres of rice fields as well as wheat, corn, alfalfa, and other crops.

Our new home was larger than any of our previous houses but still had only two bedrooms. Within a year of our moving in, Dad again converted our one-car garage into a bedroom for me. He then built a carport on the side of my bedroom like he did at our house in Chico.

Dad was an Eagle Scout when he was in high school, so he enrolled me in the Boy Scouts that fall when I was almost thirteen.

One evening in November, when I came home from my Boy Scout meeting, Dad met me at the door and Mom was crying in the background. Dad said, "Ginger's been in a fight with another dog . . . and, Dan, he's dying." I cried uncontrollably for the first time in my life. Ginger, who was nine, died that night. I had never felt so deeply hurt before. Even though my parents tried to console me, I couldn't get over the feeling that someone had just punched me in the stomach. My life-long companion was gone.

In Boy Scouts, I met my soon-to-be lifetime friend, John Maloney, when we were in eighth grade. Our friendship continued through high school, college, the Army, and our time flying for the California National Guard. We are still friends and try to see each other whenever we can.

In the fall of 1958, John and I had been working on a cooking merit badge, which we wanted to finish when our troop went on a camping trip to the Sacramento Game Refuge located just a few miles south of town. The refuge covers almost 11,000 acres of old rice fields and other grassland. Between November and February, anywhere from 500,000 to 800,000 migrating ducks in addition to around 200,000 geese can be found passing through the refuge headed south for the winter.

We set up camp in a large barren area the Fish and Game ranger had designated for our use. The plan was for John and me to provide dessert. Our scoutmasters tried to persuade us to make something that had a chance of turning out edible, but we were determined to make a lemon meringue pie in the wilderness.

After we ate our dinner and while the others were cleaning up, John took out a large cast iron Dutch oven that he had brought. He mixed the crust mixture and smeared it onto the inside of the Dutch oven and then placed the oven onto the coals of the fire to bake. Meanwhile, I beat the egg whites while John began mixing the lemon filling. I must have lost a bet to get this job! I beat those egg whites until my arm was about to fall off. Finally, they were stiff enough to use.

With the crust done, the lemon mixture was poured onto the crust and then covered with the meringue. The Dutch oven was placed back on the coals then covered with an aluminum tent which reflected the heat onto the pie. The pie baked to a beautiful golden brown, at least that's how I remember it. It was the best lemon meringue pie I have ever eaten, or maybe I wanted dessert so bad that I didn't care what it tasted like!

The following summer, our scoutmasters took us on an eighteen-mile hike into the foothills west of Willows. After all the planning, only nine out of fifteen kids agreed to go on the hike, which included John and me. The plan was to hike nine miles into a prearranged campsite where we would spend the night then hike the nine miles out the next day.

Each of us carried a forty-pound backpack that included: food, sleeping bag, a change of socks, and a knife. Every other Scout carried a two-man tent.

After driving about an hour to our starting point, we began hiking. The hike in was fairly easygoing because the trail skirted around the hills rather than going over them. I think this was more for the Scoutmasters' benefit than ours.

We hadn't walked more than a couple of miles when a couple of the younger Scouts began complaining about how hard it was, saying, "We want to go home," and "It's too hard."

One of the Scoutmasters said to the two boys, "We can't go back, but you can set up your tent right here on the trail, and we will pick you up on our way out tomorrow."

The other Scoutmaster said, "You'll also need to build a fort of logs and branches around your tent as high as you can so the bears and mountain lions won't attack and eat you during the night." Upon hearing this, the complaining stopped. When we reached the campsite, we set up our tents, stowed our gear, and after eating dinner, spent the rest of the evening working on merit badge projects and exploring the area.

Around 2:00 a.m., we were awakened by what sounded like a woman screaming. After much discussion among ourselves, we were convinced it had been one of our Scoutmasters trying to scare us.

Then our scoutmasters began yelling, "Stay in your tents and don't come out until we tell you to."

"But, what if I need to go to the bathroom?" one of the kids asked.

"Just stay in your tent. Now go to sleep." The next morning, we were still trying to figure out what the screaming was about, but the only thing we could come up with was it had to have been the Scoutmasters.

After breakfast, we packed up our gear and started hiking back to the trucks. About fifty yards from camp we came upon a dead, half-eaten fawn lying alongside the trail. Our scoutmasters then told us it had been a mountain lion we had heard during the night.

Of course, by the time we got home, our story of what had happened became somewhat embellished. John and I were never afraid at any time, but some of the younger kids had been.

By the end of our freshman year of high school, Les Engelmann, John Maloney, and I had each earned enough merit badges (twenty-one) to become Eagle Scouts. Three weeks later, the three of us went to a camp in the Sierra Mountains that resulted in our becoming members of the Order of the Arrow.

In 1960, I was fifteen and had just finished my freshman year in high school when I landed my first real job at the local A & W Root Beer stand located next to highway 99W. The Interstate (I-5) hadn't been built yet so all the traffic went through town.

My job was to keep all the supply shelves filled for the carhops and people working the counter. Other duties included washing the root beer mugs, drying them, and placing them in large freezers as well as making fresh root beer in a large twenty-gallon vat. Making root beer was my most important responsibility.

One day, I was filling the vat with water when one of the car hops called for me to come help her. I was having so much fun helping the car hop, a pretty high-school senior, that I totally forgot about the running water in back.

"Dan, where are you?" I heard the manager say. In the back room, the entire floor was covered with water from the overflowing vat. Fortunately, no damage was done because all the supplies were on racks and not directly on the floor.

I kept my job for the rest of the summer, earning $1.25 an hour and drank more root beer that summer than I have since then.

That summer I also went to work for a farmer north of town loading and stacking bales of hay in daytime temperatures that reached over one hundred degrees.

We worked from 7:00 a.m. until about 3:00 p.m. every day with an hour for lunch, during which I spent most of the time sleeping. We also were given a break mid-morning and mid-afternoon at which time the farmer gave us a cold beer to drink.

The hay by this time had already been dried and baled with the bales scattered over the field. The farmer would drive a flatbed truck beside a row of bailed hay, stopping at each bale. I would grab the bale with two large steel hooks and throw it up onto the truck bed. Another guy standing on the truck would then stack the bale on the truck. When the truck was full, we would drive back to the barn and reverse the process. The guy on the truck grabbed a bale and tossed it onto the ground, and the farmer and I dragged the bale using steel hooks into the barn and stacked it.

We were always on the alert for black widow spiders in the barn that had a tendency to jump on you if you got too close to their webs. At the end of each day, I'd come home black with dirt.

Mom used her washing machine a lot in those days.

By the time school began in September, I was more than ready to go back. My skin was a dark brown because I seldom wore a shirt while working in the sun. Even though it was hard work, I made $2.25 an hour when the going rate for high schoolers was $1.25 an hour.

One of my favorite places to go fishing was on the Middle Fork of the Feather River about twenty miles from Quincy where we used to live. During the summer of 1961 when I was sixteen, Dad and I and two of dad's friends, Jerry and Matt, took a fishing trip to that spot. Jerry and Matt, who had also been my Scoutmasters, built three Tote-Goats which were the forerunners of today's dirt bikes. The bikes had balloon-size tires, weighed about 150 pounds, and had a top speed of about ten miles an hour.

That weekend we packed up the three Goats, all our camping gear and supplies, including our gold pan, and loaded everything into two pickup trucks.

We left Willows around 4:00 a.m. on a Friday morning and arrived at our destination around 9:00 a.m. After loading all our gear onto the three Goats, we proceeded down a very narrow, steep deer trail that dropped about nine hundred feet in elevation in switchbacks to the stream below. The trip down took about forty-five minutes.

The first thing we did upon arriving at our campsite was to build a fire, then we set up our camp. We didn't bring a tent, intending to sleep under the stars. It was summer so we weren't counting on rain.

As soon as the fire had some good coals going, one of the adults filled a large metal cast-iron coffee pot with water, poured in a good amount of coffee grounds, put it on the coals and let it sit there the rest of the day. The plan was to keep adding wood now and then when one of us would pass by the campsite. At my age, keeping an eye on the coffee pot was not on my priority list of things to do. That coffee pot stayed on those coals from the time we arrived until Sunday when we packed up to leave. All they did was add water to the pot when it got low and more coffee grounds in with the old. By Sunday morning it seemed to me like the three of them were drinking mud.

This part of the river was so difficult to get to that we saw very little evidence of any other visitors. As a result, the fishing was great. Every morning after breakfast, which usually came shortly after dawn, we would head out fishing.

Jerry and Matt would usually go downstream, and Dad and I would go upstream. Dad and I only fly-fished on this trip and kept only what we could eat for lunch and dinner that day except on Sunday when we limited out. We packed the fish we brought out in ice chests filled with dry ice.

When we weren't fishing, Dad and I would look for old streambeds and dig in the dirt until we found a likely spot where gold might have been caught as we both loved to pan for gold.

Saturday morning as I was stepping over some large rocks, I heard a loud rattle. As I looked down between the rocks, I could see a rattlesnake about two feet below me. Dad suggested, "Leave it alone," which I did.

Afternoons were spent swimming in the cold water, reading, playing pinochle or napping.

Sunday morning after breakfast, we packed up our gear, including the coffee pot and gold pan, loaded up the Goats, and began our trek up the steep trail to the trucks.

About two-thirds of the way up the trail, one of the Goats broke down. Three of us drove the other two Goats to the top where the pickups were parked then walked back down to the broken Goat. While Dad carried what was left of our gear, Jerry, Matt and I pushed the disabled Goat to the top. It took us over four hours to get out of that canyon.

I don't remember whose idea it was, but instead of going directly home, we decided we would drive into Reno and do some gambling. I won two $7.50 jackpots on the nickel slot machines. I guess I was so dirty that the pit bosses couldn't tell that I was only sixteen. When we got home late Sunday night, Mom was appalled at how dirty and smelly the two of us were, but we were smiling.

SIX

The Escaping Duck Escapade

MANY A WEEKEND YOU COULD find John and me either fishing or hunting together. Our friends liked going with us because we seemed to be successful at whatever we did. I think our over-the- edge competitiveness added to our success.

David Tout, a classmate of ours, had been bugging the two of us for some time to take him duck hunting. On a Saturday in November of 1961, we said we would take him along, however, this would require him to drive his car since my dad needed to use my car, a green '53 Ford. I loved that car as basic as it was. It had a column stick shift, and an overhead six-cylinder engine.

The fact that David had a car, a blue 1960 Chevy Coupe, probably wasn't a very good reason to take him with us, but he said he wanted to go anyway.

I told John, "Who are we to disappoint him?"

We got off to a late start, so John and I decided to go road hunting. This consisted of driving up and down county roads looking for ducks in the drainage ditches that ran around the rice fields as well as checking out the various sloughs in the area.

We had been hunting a good part of the afternoon with nothing to show for our efforts. As we headed down a county road on our way home, it was starting to get dark when I looked out onto a plowed rice field (the rice had already been harvested) and saw a couple of dozen ducks landing about hundred yards from the road.

John and I told David to stop the car so we could sneak up on the ducks. David was not at all happy with this idea and said, "If you two get caught you will be in a lot of trouble. And besides, it's after shooting hours, and the field you're planning to hunt on is private property."

We would not be deterred; besides, we knew the farmer who owned the fields.

While David waited in his car, we put on our hunting vests, grabbed our shotguns, and started walking down an almost empty drainage ditch. The ditch paralleled the rice field where we had spotted the ducks landing.

After we walked about a hundred yards in a roundabout way, we climbed up on the bank of the drainage ditch. We then began crawling on our bellies over the muddy rice field toward our targets. We couldn't tell what the ducks were doing because we kept our heads down as we crawled so the ducks wouldn't see our faces and get spooked.

Our low profiles were also shielded by the rice paddy dikes in front of us. These dirt dikes are about eighteen inches high and overgrown with old rice stalks and tullies—tall grasses and cattails. After crawling over two dikes and fields, we could tell most of the ducks were on the other side of the dike we were leaning against. As we lay there, several ducks landed behind us, and one almost landed on top of John. The noise the ducks were making, quacking and flapping their wings, was so loud that we had to speak directly in each other's ear to be heard.

We both had double-barrel, side-by-side, twelve-gauge shotguns. John and I loaded our guns then put two shells in our mouths for easy reloading.

I was thinking there must be at least a hundred ducks on the other side of the dike, maybe even more by the noise they were making. From a squatting position, on cue we quickly stood up. I almost dropped my shotgun as what must have been 900 to 1,000 ducks came off the ground at the same time. It was incredible and the noise was deafening. We each emptied both barrels, reloaded, and fired again. We couldn't miss.

By then it was dark, so we laid our guns against the dike and began running around the muddy field collecting the dead and wounded ducks. By the time we found all the ducks we had shot, we counted over twenty, more than twice the daily limit for each of us! We tied the ducks onto our slings and started walking toward where we had left the car and, oh yes, David.

The ducks seemed to weigh a ton as we trudged back to the car over the muddy plowed rice field. When we got to the car, we were exhausted.

David was in a panic when he saw all the ducks we had shot. We loaded the trunk of his Coupe to the brim with the ducks, got in his car, mud and all, and headed for town.

As we were driving through town on the way to John's house, we spotted several of our friends at the local gas station. "Stop!" we both demanded. We wanted to show off all the ducks we had shot.

When we opened the trunk of the car, several wounded ducks flew out and began running around the gas station lot. John and I and our friends ran around the gas station lot chasing those ducks until we had finally corralled the four or five ducks that had escaped. I'm sure if someone had been watching, it would have brought to mind the Keystone Cops.

David drove us to John's house and quickly left after we unloaded his car. He didn't want any of the ducks. I hate to think what the inside of his car looked like between our mud-caked clothes and boots and those bloody ducks.

For the next three hours, we plucked and cleaned every one of those ducks.

David was probably terrified of being caught because he was dating a girl named Sue who just happened to be the local game warden's daughter. I don't remember David asking to go hunting with us ever again.

I finally got home about ten that night with my share of the ducks. When I told my parents everything that had happened, Mom gave me a lecture on how badly we had treated David. "You should treat others the way you would like to be treated." Dad just sat there, proudly smiling at my successful hunt. I'm not sure, but I seem to remember hearing Mom give him a lecture also.

Our friends we saw at the gas station told everyone at school, as well as several of the townspeople, about our hunting adventure. We heard later that John and I had been put on the game warden's watch list but heard no more about it.

We never ran out of fish, crawdads, quail, frog legs, pheasants, and, of course, ducks in those years.

SEVEN

Transition Years

HIGH SCHOOL FOR ME WAS an adventure. Weekdays were filled with school and school-related activities, which in those days were very few. My weekends, after my chores were done, of course, found me out of the house busy by myself or with my friends.

During my junior and senior year, I worked after school and some Saturdays at the local sporting goods store in town. My primary job was repairing bicycles in addition to stocking shelves with products. I could take a bike completely apart, clean it, repack all the bearings, and put it back together in about an hour. Of course, bikes back then didn't have all the gears and other accessories they have today.

Sometimes I rode my bike ten miles to the Sacramento River, fished most of the day, and was back for dinner, feeling it was a great day. On one of my excursions to the Sacramento River, I hooked a large fish, and after about a fifteen-minute fight, landed a five-pound, silver-side salmon.

I seldom watched television in those days probably because only three stations came in, and it was always a hassle adjusting the "rabbit ears" or maneuvering the aluminum foil that stretched between the two antennas to get a good reception. My family and I did like watching the *Ed Sullivan Show* together on Sunday nights.

More than television, I loved to get in my bedroom with the curtains closed and the lights off and listen to the radio programs like *The Shadow, The Green Hornet, The Lone Ranger, Boston Blackie,* and other adventuresome broadcasts.

On the weekends during our senior year, we'd sometimes drive over to Chico to go to a dance at the county fairgrounds. In a large building with a raised stage in the middle, live bands would play all the newest rock-n-roll hits—bands like the Beach Boys and other soon-to-be-well known bands—as well as some local bands would play. There would often be 200 to 300 kids from Chico and the surrounding towns dancing at these events.

If we had the money, we would drive over to Chico State College and listen to groups like the Kingston Trio, Peter, Paul and Mary, Simon & Garfunkel, and others. Most of these groups were new at that time, and we were hearing some of their songs for the first time. But it wouldn't be the last.

I classified myself as an average student when it came to grades. In some classes, I earned As and Bs, while in most other classes I got Cs with an occasional D.

During my senior year, I joined the school choir. The school put on a production of *Showboat* in which I sang the solo, "Old Man River." One Saturday evening in December, I sang one of the male solo parts in a modified production of the *Messiah*, a production held in the church our family attended. I also played the trombone in our school concert band.

My senior class consisted of eighty-eight students by the time I graduated from high school in June of 1962 when I was seventeen. For some reason, colleges and universities weren't breaking down my door to offer me a scholarship; I guess they weren't offering scholarships in fishing, hunting, gold mining, or bicycle repair in those days.

That summer I went to work for a lumber mill about twenty miles west of town where I "pulled chain" all summer. Pulling chain consisted of grabbing rough boards as they slid down onto long, thick, rotating chains then grabbing the boards I had been assigned to by a grader and stacking them on pallets. It was hard, dirty work, but I was paid $3.35 an hour.

The next three years, I worked various jobs in the summer as well as part-time jobs after school while attending three different junior colleges from 1962 to 1965. My grades were about the same as high school. Even though I could have stayed in one college until I earned my degree, I was restless, always looking for some new excitement and adventure. I was tired of school and wanted to "see the world." The problem was, I didn't have much money.

Some of the part-time jobs I worked at during my high school and college years were wrapping and stacking Christmas trees onto large flatbed trucks, doing yard work for local residents, washing and waxing cars, working for a building contractor, working one summer for the US Forest Service building trails, clearing brush and cutting down trees, and even selling Electrolux vacuum cleaners door to door.

On November 22, 1963, John, our friend Ron, and I went pheasant hunting. Opening day of the season wasn't scheduled to begin until the next day, but we thought we would get a head start on everyone else. Besides, we knew the farmer who owned the land where we wanted to hunt.

Around noon we headed for a local bar located along a county levy road to have lunch. When we walked into the bar, the bartender and some local farmers were staring at the television and didn't even turn their heads to look at us when we came in.

"Bill, what's going on?" Ron asked the bartender.

The bartender turned and said, "President Kennedy has been shot and killed."

The thought of someone killing the president was so unthinkable that I just sat there with everyone else listening to the news broadcasts not knowing what to say or how to respond to the news.

While attending Yuba Junior College in Marysville, California, I signed up to take a dance class. Out of some fifteen students, I was the only guy in the class. Let's just say it was a very enjoyable and memorable semester.

Sometimes I would be walking through the campus with my friends when they would hear a girl shout, "Danny, Danny," waving her arm to get my attention. The guys I ran around with kept bugging me to tell them what I had that made me so appealing to so many girls. I'd respond, "I just have that special magnetism girls are attracted to." Actually, the girls were all my fellow dance classmates. Maybe they liked me because I was a fairly good dancer as my mother had taught me how to dance.

The following year, I transferred to American River College just outside of Sacramento and moved in with three of my high school classmates, one being John. This would turn out to be a year of great change for me.

We were all living on limited budgets, but we'd buy T-bone steaks when they came on sale at the grocery store near our apartment. These steaks would come with about a half an inch of fat around the edges. We fried the steaks in a cast-iron skillet, making sure the fat was cooked well. After removing the steaks, we then placed thick slices of bread in the skillet to soak up the grease and fried the bread to a golden brown. The bread was flavorful and delicious. Fortunately, none of us died from clogged arteries, though I wouldn't recommend this recipe as a regular meal choice.

One afternoon, the four of us decided to have a beer at a local bar called the Tropicana, a real dive and nothing like the Tropicana in Las Vegas. We liked this place because the afternoon bartender never asked us for our ID. That afternoon, we were the only customers in the bar as a tall, beautiful woman with long black hair and a guy wearing a sheep skin vest sang and played a guitar. Years later we were convinced they were Sonny and Cher. They were probably just starting out and were playing wherever they could find work.

During the spring of 1965, I worked for a nursery in Carmichael, a suburb of Sacramento. when I wasn't attending classes. My goal was to save enough money so I could travel to Tahiti or some other exotic place. I didn't know it, but the US Government was in the process of preparing their own plans for my life.

"We're all getting drafted!" John informed me one day. We were single and didn't have the grades to keep us out of the draft. This didn't seem fair because John's dad was on the local draft board, and after all, John was his son, and I was John's friend. We had carefully reasoned that John's dad should convince the state draft board to place us at the bottom of the draft list. But that didn't change the draft board's decision.

John's dad told us in no uncertain terms, "If you don't do something soon, you are going to be drafted."

Upset by this unwelcome news, John and I discussed all our options and decided there were only two available to us. One was finding a single girl within a week, woo her with flowers and sweet talk, propose to her, drive to Reno, get married while trying to assure our parents that we had not completely lost all our mental faculties.

Two was enlisting in the military branch of our choice. Since we weren't totally convinced we could find any two honorable girls at such short notice who would have jumped at the great opportunity our plan offered, we concluded the only option available to us was to enlist.

While I worked in the lumber mill that summer, John worked for the US Forestry in what they called "heli-tack" operations. Whenever there was a lightning strike or other small fire detected, a helicopter was dispatched with John and one other person on board. The helicopter would hover over or near the fire while John and the other person would jump out and try to put out or contain the fire before it got out of control.

John's pilot told him about the Army helicopter school.

Taking the pilot's advice, in the fall of 1965, John and I drove to the local US Army recruiter's office in Sacramento where we told the recruiter, "We want to sign up for helicopter school."

The recruiter told us, "I don't have any information about the school. It's fairly new. I'll get back to you."

About a week later, the recruiter called us about the school, and we arranged a time to drive back down to Sacramento to sign our enlistment papers as well as the helicopter school enrollment papers.

A week later, we boarded a bus headed to Oakland, California. We spent the day taking a preliminary physical and a battery of written and oral exams which we had to pass to be admitted to helicopter school.

A couple of weeks after that, the recruiter called us both to say, "You passed all the tests." He then scheduled us to take a flight physical at the Presidio in San Francisco.

We drove to San Francisco for our flight physical. Back home after the physical, I told my dad that my four-plus-hour flight physical was, "So thorough that the doctors and nurses probed areas of my body I didn't know I had." Again, we both passed.

November 16, 1965, John and I boarded a Boeing 707 in San Francisco heading to Fort Polk, Louisiana to begin two months of basic training. I had never flown before in any type of aircraft. Scared and excited, I was trying to look as cool as a twenty-one-year-old guy should look on his way to the adventure of a lifetime.

EIGHT

Learning to Fly

THAT NOVEMBER AND DECEMBER AT Fort Polk was cold and wet. The company John and I were assigned to turned out to be easy duty compared to other basic training companies. One of the reasons was that 40 percent of our class were on their way to helicopter school. Also, our company commander was from my town, Chico. In two months of training, I pulled KP once, guard duty once, and only had to march on a ten-mile forced march once.

Two weeks after beginning our basic training, John got his draft notice in the mail. He had a difficult time convincing the State of California draft board that he was already in the Army.

One Saturday afternoon, some five hundred basic training troops were marched into a large auditorium and then entertained for over an hour by Louis Armstrong and his band. I had never heard such talented musicians before and found it an incredible experience. Louis Armstrong was mesmerizing.

Upon graduating from basic training, I was assigned to the basic helicopter school at Fort Walters in Mineral Wells, Texas. I was promoted to the rank of E-5 while in school.

My flight instructor was a civilian with two middle fingers missing on his right hand as they were shot off while he served in the Korean War. Besides flying, he taught me many new swear words. He didn't really teach me the words, it was more like he screamed those words at me when I messed up, or he thought I wasn't paying attention. I am 6'2" tall, and he was about 5'8"; I was sure he was going to kill me.

The helicopter I was trained in was an OH-23 Hiller. In those five months, he taught me and his three other students things about flying a helicopter that many of the other students who had military instructors missed out on. I was one of the first students in our class to solo.

During the first day of academic classes, our civilian aerodynamics instructor made this opening statement: "Gentlemen, it is important for you to understand that, aerodynamically, a helicopter is not supposed to fly." There were about 180 students in that classroom, and I'm sure I wasn't the only one who was wondering, *What in the world was I thinking of when I signed up to fly helicopters?*

He then added, "As you are flying around the sky, never forget, the only thing keeping your helicopter from crashing is you."

After the five months of basic helicopter training, we were assigned to the advanced helicopter school at Fort Rucker, Alabama. A few days before graduating from basic helicopter school, our company commander announced there were too many in our class so some of the students would proceed to Fort Rucker while the rest would remain at Fort Walters and join the class behind us.

John and I volunteered to stay behind and go with the next class, but they sent John on ahead anyway. So, my friend John and I were separated. During that month, my days consisted of flying, lying around the barracks, reading, and sleeping.

Advance training at Fort Rucker was now more practical and intense. We were now flying UH-1 A, B, and D (Huey) models. Occasionally, we flew the C or what was called the "Charlie model," which was mainly used for our gunship training.

After four months at Fort Rucker I graduated from helicopter school with orders sending me to Vietnam, wherever that was.

Because I was to leave from Travis Air Force Base in northern California, I took a week of leave to visit my parents who lived on Lake Almanor located at 4,500 feet in the Sierra Mountains. It was then January of 1967, and I was twenty-two years old.

Mom took my assignment especially hard. My dad had been wounded and almost lost his life in WW II, so she was especially fearful I would lose my life flying this dangerous aircraft.

For me, however, the old saying, "Ignorance is bliss" applied. I knew very little about Vietnam or what to expect when I got there. It didn't seem to be a big deal to me. I was still excited by the fact that I was now a qualified helicopter pilot with just over two hundred hours of flight time to my credit.

On January 6, after my time with Mom and Dad, I took a bus to San Francisco where I met up with Tom McKay, a fellow helicopter pilot from Maine.

The Boston Celtics happened to be playing the San Francisco Warriors at the Cow Palace and Tom wanted to see the game. As we rode the taxi to the Cow Palace, the taxi driver informed, "I hear that game's been sold out for weeks." Tom wanted to try anyway.

When we arrived wearing our Army uniforms, I asked the lady behind the ticket counter if there were any tickets available, she said, "Sorry, the game is sold out."

A man in a three-piece suit standing behind the counter asked, "Are the two of you based nearby?"

I said, "No, sir, we just graduated from helicopter flight school and are on our way to Vietnam. My friend Tom is from Maine and a big Celtics fan."

"Please wait here," the man said.

He was gone about ten minutes. When he returned, he said something to the ticket agent then came out to where we were standing. He handed us two free tickets and said, "Please follow me." We followed him into the packed stadium, and he seated us right behind the Celtic bench. We could almost touch the players! You would have thought they had given Tom the keys to Fort Knox. Unfortunately for Tom, the Celtics lost by two points.

On January 9, 1967, Tom and I boarded a Boeing 707 for a long and tiring flight to Vietnam. After arriving in Saigon, Tom and I parted ways, and I was immediately put on a C-130 transport that flew me and about forty other personnel, along with several pallets of supplies and parts, north to An Khe where the headquarters of the 1st Cavalry Division was based. We arrived at An Khe around 11:00 p.m. Eight other pilots and I were driven to an operations company and ushered into a hooch (hut).

Before leaving Fort Rucker, my flight instructor had told me to expect hot and humid weather in Vietnam. But when I got off the plane at An Khe, it was cold and raining because An Khe is located at an elevation of 2,300 feet in the mountains.

We reported to the captain in charge of assigning each of the pilots to various 1st Cav companies. All the pilots had been pre-assigned except for me and one other pilot. The captain asked the two of us, "Which one of you would like to be assigned to a gun company?"

I had flown a training gunship at Fort Rucker and thought they were a lot of fun to fly. Dad had spent a lot of time teaching me how to shoot different weapons when I was younger, so I volunteered.

It seemed odd to me at the time when the captain looked at me very seriously and said, "Are you sure this is what you want to do?"

I said, "Yes," having no idea what I had just volunteered for.

I found out later that flying Huey gunships was one of the most dangerous flying jobs in Vietnam. Also, gun companies rarely assigned pilots to their company right out of flight school. But the company I was assigned to was in desperate need of pilots because they had lost several pilots who had been either wounded or killed over the previous several months.

The next three days were spent flying training flights with my platoon leader. On the third day, we went on an assault mission north of An Khe where we encountered heavy resistance from the enemy. During the assault, a small observation plane was shot down, and several enemy bullets hit our helicopter.

Up until that time in my short-lived, sheltered life, I had never experienced someone shooting a gun at me, let alone trying to kill me. As I lay on my cot that night, mulling over what had happened that day, I realized I was in a dangerous survival situation. My defense mechanisms kicked in, and my whole mindset changed from a happy-go-lucky, carefree, life-is-to-have-fun attitude, to a Rambo, it's-them-or-me attitude.

In the months and years to come, other pilots often told me I scared them to death when they flew with me or flew as my wingman. They said it was because of the way I flew with such abandon, showing no fear in any situation, and often pushing the helicopter's capabilities to the edge. But they also liked flying with me because I was determined to come back, no matter what.

On the fifth day after my arrival in Vietnam, I was flown north to LZ Hammond, a base near the South China Sea where I received more combat training.

A month after my arrival at Hammond, our entire combat division was moved further north to LZ English in the Bong Song Valley. LZ English was a large, raised mound of barren ground in the middle of a valley covered with many rice fields and several small Vietnamese villages.

There was an airstrip, MASH unit, and several hundred helicopters including the men, materials, and supplies to support those helicopter units. Our helicopter company was located about a quarter of a mile from the airstrip.

Living with three other pilots in a tent, each of us with different daily flight schedules as well as helicopters flying in and out all day and night, resulted in many interrupted nights of sleep. The floor of our tent was dirt; our luxurious bed was a good old Army cot. We were allotted a cold, three-minute shower once every three or four days.

In March, I was promoted to aircraft commander and fire team leader, a position normally held by a commissioned officer, but we were short on commissioned officers at that time.

✈ NINE ✈

Into the Fire

ON APRIL 8, 1967, WE were in a fierce battle in a valley northeast of LZ English known as the "Valley of Death" (not the same infamous Valley of Death from a 1965 battle). The battle had lasted most of the day. Several hours into the conflict I was coming around, ready to make another run at an enemy position, when a rocket came out of a building, hit, and blew up another helicopter.

I was one of the last helicopters to leave the valley. As I was gaining some altitude to leave, I got a distress call on my FM radio from some troops on the ground. One of their sergeants had been seriously wounded and needed immediate transport to the MASH unit at English.

Gunships had standing orders not to land and pick up people on the ground because they are already heavy due to the armament and weapons they carry and normally take a longer distance to take off than other helicopters. But by then, there were no other helicopters in the area.

Low on fuel and having expended most of my ordinance, I made the decision to go in and pick up the wounded soldier. There was still a great deal of fighting going as we approached the landing area. As I got close, I saw a barbed wire fence surrounding the area in which I was planning to land. There would be just enough space for the helicopter to set down in.

It was dark, but I didn't turn on my landing lights because it would have given the enemy a great target to shoot at. With my crew chief and gunner guiding me, I set the helicopter down in the small clearing. As soon as my skids touched the ground, men came running out with the wounded soldier. With help from my crew chief and gunner, the men laid him on the hard steel floor of the helicopter, and I immediately brought the helicopter to a hover and took off barely clearing the fence.

I called ahead to let the doctors know we were coming in with the wounded soldier. Since gunships didn't carry wounded soldiers, I had never landed at the MASH helipad at LZ English. LZ English had very limited lighting at night to reduce the visibility of strategic areas to the enemy. As I approached the airfield, I relied on the airfield tower operators to direct me to the MASH landing pad, which I finally found.

As soon as we landed, orderlies came running out with a stretcher only to come to a screeching halt when they saw we were a gunship. My crew chief and gunner waved them forward assuring them that it was okay to step in front of the M60 machine guns and rocket pods.

I assume the wounded soldier survived.

I have left out many of the events of that day when I flew almost eight hours. Because of my actions, I was awarded the Air Medal for Valor.

When I finally got back to my unit, after refueling and rearming, I plopped down on my cot and didn't wake up until twelve hours later when my platoon leader woke me up to fly another mission.

On August 9, 1967, I was part of one of the largest assaults of the war up to that time. There was a large area in the mountains that the North Vietnamese and Viet Cong controlled. Several aircraft had been shot down entering this area and many men had been wounded or lost their lives trying to take control of it.

In this assault, which had been planned for weeks, there were a large number of "slicks" (troop-carrying helicopters), numerous gunships, and several hundred troops involved.

The area was prepped by Air Force jets then by our gunships. The fighting was fierce and lasted most of the day. I returned to our base to rearm and refuel several times during the day.

At one point after dropping off their troops, a group of troop transport helicopters were pinned down under heavy enemy fire. Their flight commander began desperately calling for any gunship in the area to give them cover so they could take off.

Seeing this happening, I flew at a low level laying down suppressive fire in addition to launching a salvo of rockets pinning down the enemy and enabling the helicopters to take off without getting blown out of the sky.

During that whole day, my helicopter did not sustain one bullet strike despite all the fierce fighting. A great deal happened that day and for my actions I was awarded the Distinguished Flying Cross.

When I finally got back to base and shut down, my platoon leader who was also in that engagement said to me, "Dan, I saw tracer bullets going through your helicopter." After a thorough inspection, there was not a single bullet hole found on my helicopter.

Years later, Aunt Margaret, my dad's older sister and I were having a conversation about the war. When we put together dates to the action I just described, she said, "About 3:00 in the morning, I woke up with this overwhelming dread that you were in grave danger, and I was to get out of bed, get on my knees, and pray for you, which I did." I believe her obedience to that prompting to pray for me saved my life and the lives of my crew.

On September 19, 1967, our company was deployed on a mission to attack an enemy position in the mountains southwest of LZ English. The enemy was entrenched in a hillside at an elevation of 3,000 feet above sea level. After completing our mission, as we were heading back to base, I decided to stay at 3,000 feet because the temperature was only ninety degrees as opposed to 110 degrees in the valley.

I was at the controls since my co-pilot was new to our unit and had never flown a combat mission in a gunship before. Suddenly, there was a loud bang, the helicopter lurched forward, and began an uncontrollably tight turn descending toward the ground at a rapid rate of speed. I tried to right the helicopter, thinking we had been hit by an enemy rocket. My crew chief yelled, "Mr. Miller, the left cargo door has come off and hit the left stabilizer wing on the tail and then hit the tail rotor. We have a complete tail rotor failure!"

As we were spinning out of control toward the ground, I began doing everything I could think of to gain control of the helicopter, but nothing seemed to help. My co-pilot panicked and began grabbing at the controls, which added to the difficulty of the situation. Finally, about 400 feet above the ground, I was able to stop the spinning. We were now flying forward, but at a very dangerous angle and shaking violently. Numerous warning lights were flashing, indicating system failures. It was all I could do to keep the helicopter from crashing.

Our flight level was now 150 feet above the ground. Flying that helicopter was like what I thought riding a bucking bronco must be.

I was calling "Mayday" on the radio when another helicopter informed me, "I saw you go down. I'm trailing you." He began sending messages forward to the closest airfield ordering them to prepare crash trucks and emergency personnel for our anticipated landing.

We still had several hundred rounds of 7.62mm ammunition and several rockets on board. So, I made the decision to fly over the South China Sea about five miles from the airstrip I was planning to land on and dump the rest of our ordinance into the sea. That burned off additional fuel that could ignite if we crashed. At this point, this seemed to be our only option.

As I approached the dirt airstrip, I had difficulty lining up my approach with the runway because of the cockeyed angle the helicopter was flying without any tail rotor control. Keeping my airspeed at about 80 knots helped keep the helicopter from going into another spin. On my final approach to the runway, I realized I was not lined up properly, so I nosed the helicopter over to build up more speed. This meant we were now flying about fifty feet over the ground.

My crew chief said, "People on the ground are running every which way to get out of the way. They must think we are going to crash." I brought the helicopter around once more, lined it up with the runway, and began my approach.

As the helicopter touched the runway the left skid hit a rock. They had failed to warn me that the runway was in the process of being graded.

Hitting the rock veered us to the right causing us to hit the ground hard, bouncing us into a long mound of dirt that ran along the edge and length of the runway. We hit the mound of dirt, and the helicopter flipped onto its left side. When the rotor blades hit the ground, dirt, rocks, and pieces of metal went flying everywhere, and the transmission was torn from its mountings.

When the helicopter finally came to a stop, I began turning off the fuel, electrical, and other systems. While this was going on, my crew chief and gunner had to pull my co-pilot off me because he had fallen on top of me when he unbuckled his harness.

The helicopter was totaled, but none of us was seriously injured. We all walked away with minor cuts and bruises.

I have a picture of that helicopter in my office on which I have written the Bible verse that speaks about angels: "Are they not all ministering spirits, sent out to render service for the sake of those who will inherit salvation" (Heb. 1:14).

At the time, this event seemed like just another lucky break in my life. Years later, I realized it was the Lord taking control of the situation in response to the many prayers being offered on my behalf.

I was awarded the Army Commendation Medal for my actions in saving the lives of my crew.

Two days later, I was back flying combat missions.

The heat, humidity, dirty living conditions and numerous combat missions were taking a toll on my mind and body that I didn't realize at the time. I had lost touch with reality. Even though I received many encouraging letters from my parents and others, my thoughts became darker and darker. My whole focus was on flying combat missions.

⇒ TEN ⇒

Living through It

THAT SUMMER, TIRED OF LIVING in a tent, Milo, one of my tent mates and I decided to build ourselves a hooch. We began collecting wooden rocket boxes, taking them apart, saving the wood, and straightening the nails we had pulled out. We also began saving old but usable ponchos and tents. What we didn't have were beams to nail the boards to. When I told my platoon leader our plan, he said that the engineers back at An Khe had all kinds of lumber.

One day, Milo and I had a day off, so we hopped a ride to An Khe on one of the Huey supply helicopters. We took with us an AK-47 Russian assault rifle and some other weapons we had confiscated on various occasions to trade with the engineers. As soon as we saw the reaction of the engineers when we showed them the AK-47, we knew we were going to get whatever we wanted.

The supply helicopter pilots agreed to transport our goods back to LZ English. Our trade negotiations netted us ten, 10-foot 4 x 4s, four 100-pound sacks of dry concrete and a roll of metal screening. The 4 x 4s were sticking out each side of the helicopter, which challenged the pilot's flying ability.

One day, when we both weren't flying, we built a 10-foot by 10-foot hooch about 1 foot above the ground to keep us dry during the monsoons. We framed in the window openings and covered them with the screening material. We covered the roof and the awnings over the openings with old, glued-together ponchos and tents. The awnings could be lowered tight against the screened openings to keep out the rain.

We were now living in a mansion. Pilots from other companies would come by and make drawings of our construction so they could build better living accommodations themselves. Since gun companies were the only units to have access to rocket boxes, this became a great bargaining tool with the slick pilots.

Shortly after we completed our project, my platoon leader came to me and said, "How do you think this looks, you living in luxury and your company commander still living in a tent?"

Without hesitation, we began collecting rocket boxes again and bartering for more stuff we could trade with the engineers.

About a month later, with all the wood, including 4 x 4s, screening, old tents, and cement we needed, we got together the pilots as well as some enlisted personnel and built our CO an A-frame house that included a front porch. I could do no wrong after that as far as my CO was concerned.

My platoon leader went on R & R to visit his wife in Hawaii that summer. When he returned, he told me he had purchased two acres of land on the Big Island of Hawaii. He had visited the property and said it was on level ground and in a great location. He gave me the information on the company that was selling the property. Within a month, I was the proud owner of two acres of land in Hawaii, which cost me $1,999 an acre.

The first week in December of 1967, I was called into my CO's office. He said, "Mr. Miller, I've received one allocation for a pilot to be sent to Ben Hue to attend the new Cobra flight school. The school runs from December 18 to January 3. I've decided to send you."

There was one catch, however. I had to extend my Vietnam tour of duty for another six months, which I agreed to do. I had already put in for a tour of duty in Germany, but my CO thought this would supersede that request.

Arriving at Ben Hue, I was driven to a secured base where I lived in an air-conditioned room by myself. I ate great hot meals every day, could take a hot shower every day and twice a day if I wanted, and went to classes in an air-conditioned classroom. I was in heaven.

The AH-1G Cobra attack helicopter was new to the Army and was considered one of the fastest and most heavily armed helicopters in the world at that time. At fifty-three feet in length with a fuselage of only three feet wide, not including the wing stores, it cruised fully loaded at 140 to 150 knots. The maneuverability of the Cobra was incredible. It carried almost twice the armament of our other gunships.

After completing two long weeks of intense classroom and flight training, I graduated from Cobra school.

As I was getting off the transport helicopter to return to my unit, the company clerk came running up and said, "You are to report to the company commander immediately."

My CO was furious, not with me, but with the Army. It seems that they had cut orders for me to be sent to Germany and refused to rescind those orders even though I had signed up to extend my tour. My Cobra training, however, would not be lost.

The year of 1967 was long and hot in more ways than one. I have left out many events of that year. How I came out unscathed was a mystery to me at the time. I chocked it up to just plain old good luck. At the end of one year, I had flown over 390 combat missions. In addition to the Distinguished Flying Cross, Air Medal for Valor, and the Commendation Medal, I was awarded thirty-three air medals as well as various campaign medals.

At times during my tour, I flew two, three, or more missions in one day. Often, I would fly eight or more hours in a day. On May 24, 1967, I flew seven different missions logging over twelve hours of flight time, three hours of that time at night.

The war had hardened me. Knowing the chances of my not coming home on any given day caused me to have an all-or-nothing mindset. I often flew as if that day was the last day of my life and put my crew and wingman into situations that were extremely more dangerous than normal.

I never had any desire to take drugs and seldom drank liquor in Vietnam because I wanted to be in complete control of my faculties. I read more books that year than I had up to that point in my life.

On January 8, 1968, I left Vietnam. On my way to Germany, I took a couple of days to visit Mom and Dad in California. Dad noticed how withdrawn and quiet I was, the opposite of the way I used to be. He told me several years later, "You had changed so much your mother told me you weren't the happy-go-lucky son she once knew." She was deeply grieved seeing the effect the war had on me.

I didn't realize at the time how dramatically the war had changed me.

⌐ ELEVEN ⌐

Flying the Brass

IT WAS EARLY MORNING OF January 12, 1968, when I arrived in Frankfurt, Germany. From there I took a train to Stuttgart then a cab to Nelligan Army Base where I would be stationed with the 129th Aviation Company for the next fifteen months. My new CO assigned me to a VIP unit within the company, which meant I spent most of my time at the airfield rather than at our company headquarters like most of the other officers.

A few weeks after arriving in Germany, I was promoted to the rank of Chief Warrant Officer-2.

Our helicopter flight operations, maintenance facility, and helicopters were located at the Stuttgart airport. German aviation, such as Lufthansa and other commercial airlines, were located on one side of the airfield and the US Air Force and Army VIP units on the other.

My primary job was flying the command staff of the Seventh Corp. One of my favorite duties was to fly the Seventh Corp commander, a three-star general. He was the Army commander over all southern Germany. Several times during my tour, I flew the general into very secretive and secure bases.

During my tour in Germany, I earned my instrument rating and became an instructor pilot in the UH-1 and CH-34 helicopters.

My duty during those months, to put it mildly, was cushy. I lived in a German town, not on the base, and rarely spent any time at our company offices. I had a great deal of free time because I essentially flew when scheduled by the Seventh Corp. From time to time, when not flying for them, I trained other pilots how to fly the CH-34 and gave new pilots their orientation training.

The CH-34 is a large helicopter capable of carrying up to eighteen combat-ready troops. The pilots sit high above the cargo bay. The engine has nine large pistons about the size of a gallon can and is noisier than most helicopters.

In the summer of 1968, there was an international air show at Stuttgart. The US Army had volunteered a CH-34 helicopter to carry ten German parachutists for a sky diving exhibition at the show, and I was selected to fly the mission.

With the parachutists and their gear loaded, I took off along with my co-pilot and crew chief. It took some time, but I finally reached the jumping out altitude of 10,000 feet. As I approached the jump-out point over the airfield, the main seal on the rotor broke. The rotor brake is located above and a little to the left of my head. When the seal failed, hot hydraulic fluid began splashing down over me and into the cargo bay beneath me where my crew chief and the ten parachutists were located.

I yelled to my crew chief over the intercom, "We're going down, get them out." He quickly opened the cargo door and yelled at the jumpers, "Ride down with us or get out *now*." All of them could see the hydraulic fluid splashing down into the cargo bay. As one, they dove out of the helicopter so fast I had to quickly adjust my attitude in order to keep the helicopter from going over on its side.

We were about ten miles from the Stuttgart airport where we were stationed. I called a Mayday, made a fast descent to that airfield, and made an emergency landing. The helicopter didn't sustain any other problems or damage; everything else was in good working order. My flight suit was drenched in hydraulic fluid, I had a few minor burns, but other than that, everyone else was fine. I assumed the skydivers put on a good show.

A late afternoon in December of 1968, I was called into the flight commander's office. He told me that I had been selected to fly a special mission to the NATO training base on the German/Czechoslovakia border east of Nuremburg.

The Cold War was in full swing and relations between the West and Russia were extremely tense. This would be about a two-hour flight that would stretch my fuel capacity to the limit, and the weather was predicted to be anything but ideal.

I selected a co-pilot and crew chief. After making sure everything was ready, full fuel tanks, inspections completed, survival gear stowed, flight plan filed and weather checked, we took off and flew over to Patch, the Seventh Corp command headquarters. We landed on the Patch soccer field, our normal landing site.

I was met by an officer and four armed guards. After receiving my permission, the guards proceeded to load a small safe onto the helicopter that my crew chief secured to the floor. The officer took me aside and informed me, "The safe contains top secret documents." He also said, "It's imperative the safe be delivered to the NATO training base as soon as possible. You are not to set down anywhere other than a secure military base and only if it is an emergency." He then gave me special secure radio frequencies and codes and told me that I was to maintain constant contact with the command center throughout my flight.

Two of the guards were to go with us, each carrying a loaded M-16 rifle and a 45-caliber pistol. By the time my briefing from the officer was over, the guards had already boarded the helicopter.

I asked the guards, "Is there a round in the chamber of your weapons?"

They replied in the affirmative.

I said, "Please clear the chamber of your weapons." When they refused, I ordered them off the aircraft.

I called the officer in charge over and told him, "We are going to encounter bad weather and turbulence on the way. I am not about to take a chance of one of them panicking and accidently dropping his weapon on the floor and have it go off." After surviving a year in Vietnam, I wasn't about to get shot in Germany.

Knowing that I had been hand selected by the command staff to fly this mission, the officer ordered the two guards to clear their weapons. I instructed my crew chief to keep an eye on the two guards because I didn't think they had flown in a helicopter before by the way they were acting. This was going to be one hairy ride.

At 2100 hours, we took off from Patch with the outside temperature registering minus nine degrees Celsius.

East of Nuremburg and about ten miles from the Czech boarder, there is an invisible barrier called the ADIZ (Air Defense Identification Zone). Aircraft are not allowed to pass through this barrier without receiving permission from the military command that controls the area. From the time an aircraft enters this area, it must maintain a strict flight path in addition to airspeed and altitude to its destination.

As we passed Nuremburg, I was given permission to enter the ADIZ as well as the flight path I was to follow, which I had flown on many previous occasions.

The weather conditions were deteriorating rapidly as we passed Nuremburg. My crew chief told me our two guards were getting very fidgety.

Suddenly, rime ice began forming at a fast rate up the entire length of the windshield. I put the heater defrosters on full, but they had little effect. I called military command requesting a lower altitude, but they refused to give it to me. The windshield was almost completely covered with ice by this time. I dropped my airspeed from ninety to sixty knots. Even though it was freezing outside, I dropped my door window and stuck my head out the window to see where I was going. My co-pilot began to call out airspeed, altitude, and heading every few seconds. We were flying almost blind.

While my co-pilot worked the collective, which controls our altitude, I maneuvered the cyclic which controls the attitude of the helicopter. I knew ice must be forming on the rotor blades and fuselage. If too much accumulated, the weight would cause us to crash. Even though it was freezing outside, my crew chief opened the cargo door on his side to help me see where we were going.

Again, I called military command, however, this time I *told* them what was happening. I said, "I am dropping down to 200 feet AGL (above ground level), or we are going to crash."

They gave permission to do so.

My crew chief told me that the faces of our two brave guards were whiter than the snow outside.

Dropping down to 200 feet and with the defrosters going full blast the ice began to slowly disappear. Five minutes later we were on final approach to the airfield.

After shutting down and with all the proper documents signed and identifications verified with my list of authorized recipients of the safe, I ordered the guards to release the safe. I could see where ice had formed on the rotor blades as well as a good part of the fuselage.

I got to bed after midnight, exhausted from one of the hairiest flights I have flown, Vietnam being the exception. All of us, including the two guards, returned to Stuttgart the next day on an uneventful flight home.

As I lived in an apartment in a German town I seldom ate on base. I loved the German food and enjoyed sleeping under heavy down comforters in the winter. Oktoberfest when thousands of people would gather under huge tents drinking beer and singing songs was also a treat. Everyone seemed to forget any troubles they may have been going through while getting together to have a good time.

One of my favorite pastimes was to play foosball in a local *gasthaus*. I had some great teachers and became very good at this "sport." Many years in the future, I had the privilege of playing several games of foosball with Seattle Seahawks Steve Largent, Jim Zorn, and another Seahawk, whose name I have since forgotten. Jim and I teamed up and won every match. (I couldn't resist including this.)

During my tour, I spent a week in Switzerland with a high school classmate as well as a week at the home of the attaché to the American Embassy in Rome whose daughter I was seeing at the time.

I felt rich because I was drawing good pay and the exchange rate was four German marks to one US dollar. I visited many German towns as well as other countries during my tour. My sister and a girlfriend of hers came over to tour Europe, and I took time off to spend a couple of days with them.

During the first week in May of 1969, I received orders returning me to Vietnam. These were not your ordinary orders. They were typed on green stationery with a handwritten note reading, "Mr. Miller, the Army is required to maintain 25 percent experienced pilots in Vietnam, and your qualifications as an AH-1G Attack Helicopter pilot and as an experienced gunship pilot is needed."

I thought they had made a mistake because I had just over six months till I was due to be discharged from the Army. I also had very important flying responsibilities as a VIP pilot so I just couldn't leave—at least that was my carefully considered thinking.

I immediately ran upstairs to the Air Force operations center where I got on their direct phone line to the Pentagon. Upon reaching the Pentagon, I asked for the warrant officer division. A Chief Warrant Officer Williams answered my call. I explained my position, and he responded by saying, "I sympathize with your plea, Mr. Miller, but your orders were issued by a higher authority than I have." He let me know that he was going back for his second tour in Vietnam also. "Is there someone else I can speak with?" I asked.

Less than thirty days later I found myself on another Boeing 707 headed back to Vietnam.

⩊ TWELVE ⩊

Back in Vietnam

ARRIVING IN SAIGON THE FIRST part of June 1969, was a
shock. As I stepped off the plane, the humid one hundred-degree heat
hit me like a blast in the face. It felt as if I had never left. This time,
however, instead of living in a tent, I would be housed in a highly secure
compound, living in an air-conditioned room, the same complex I lived
in while attending Cobra school.

I was assigned to the 334th Aviation Company. The company
maintained twenty-one Cobra attack helicopters and two UH-H Hueys.
On each Huey was mounted a 50-caliber machine gun and a large,
high-intensity light used for night missions patrolling the Delta rivers.

Within a week, I was made an aircraft commander and fire team
leader. I was, for the most part, on call twenty-four hours a day, seven
days a week, to support ground troops when they encountered the enemy.

I didn't actually fly every day. When called, our operations would
usually dispatch two Cobras, and at times four Cobras, to the conflict
to attack the enemy positions, protecting the troops on the ground. In
addition to our day operations, we also ran night ops where we would

patrol the rivers and other waterways, searching for enemy watercraft then engaging and destroying them.

On June 28 as I was relaxing in my nice air-conditioned room, there was a knock on my door. When I opened it, our company clerk was standing there and informed me that I was to report to the battalion headquarters Ready Room immediately. I had never been to a meeting at battalion HQ. When I asked him what this was about, he said, "I don't know, Sir; you will be told when you get there."

As I was walking to the meeting, several other pilots were on the way there also. There were seven of us, three of whom were aircraft commanders and fire team leaders. When we arrived at HQ, we were escorted into the building with two armed guards carrying M-16s posted outside the doors.

Now I, along with some of the others, didn't always fly by the book and tended to ignore regulations when in our opinion the situation warranted it, so this meeting had me a little concerned.

Three men dressed in black three-piece suits ordered us to take a seat along with our commanding officer who was already present. Seeing men in three-piece suits was a little odd because the temperature outside was over one hundred degrees and the air conditioning did little to lower the temperature inside the building.

The man in charge introduced himself and the other two men as United States Secret Service agents. He thanked us for coming then said, "If you were asked to protect the president of the United States, would you be willing, without question, to protect the president with your life?"

I thought this was a ridiculous question because we risked our lives everyday protecting American combat troops in the field whom we didn't know and would probably never know, except we knew they were Americans.

All of us swore we would do everything in our power and ability to protect the president.

We were then sworn to secrecy as to what we were about to hear. After some preliminary statements, the agent informed us that in two days the president would be making a surprise visit to Vietnam. We had been selected to fly four Cobras as his protection.

Two UH-1H helicopters would carry the president along with a couple of other dignitaries, several Secret Service agents, and a couple of news reporters. The general news media and others would not be informed of this visit until it was over. The president planned to visit two bases where he would award medals to some of the soldiers and speak to the troops.

Each of our Cobras was fully loaded with a full complement of rockets and 8,000 rounds of 7.62mm ammunition that would feed the mini-guns (six-barrel Gatling guns) that could fire 4,000 rounds a minute.

On the day of the president's visit, we took off from Ben Hue and flew to Saigon, about a five-minute flight at a speed of 150 knots. There we rendezvoused with the president's two Hueys.

We flew protection as the president visited the two bases. After about an hour and half, we escorted them back to Saigon where everyone boarded Air Force One and went on their way.

After we got back to base at Ben Hue, I said to one of the other pilots, "Well, I'm glad nothing unexpected happened. On the other hand, it's kind of disappointing we didn't get shot at so we could attack the enemy's position and save the president's life."

It was privilege to have been selected by the Secret Service for this assignment. The next day I was back flying combat missions.

I rarely flew escort for troop assault missions because those companies had their own gunships. One day, I was asked to take two Cobras in support of another Cobra company based thirty miles from Ben Hue and who were short on aircraft. There were the two of us and one Cobra from the company we were supporting.

Our job was to meet up with ten slicks from the company that was to extract about sixty ground troops. We arrived at our destination about twenty-five minutes later. The slicks then flew into the LZ (Landing Zone), landed, and began picking up the ground troops. This was taking place while our three Cobras circled the LZ.

Suddenly, the commander of the slick company called out, "We're receiving fire; we're receiving fire, ten o'clock!"

I happened to be coming around just in time to see the enemy's position. I radioed our flight leader and with his permission, took immediate control of the flight. I then gave quick instructions to the other two Cobra pilots. All this took place within a couple of seconds.

Standing my Cobra on its nose, I dove at the enemy's position unleashing a salvo of rockets. The enemy broke off its assault, and all ten slicks including the three of us and all the troops retuned to base without any loss of life or aircraft.

I got to know one of the air force pilots stationed at the air force base at Ben Hue. He was one of two U-2 pilots. He liked coming over to our officer's club because the officer in charge of our club had a way of getting some of the best entertainment available. He was a little wild and didn't seem big on following the rules by the stories he told us about his life.

One day, one of our pilots gave him a ride in a Cobra. After his flight, he told us, "Flying in that Cobra scared me to death." We thought his flying the U-2 was scary.

On another day, I was flying a mission west of Ben Hue when, suddenly, sparks started flying out of the circuit breaker panel next to my right arm. Flames came up out of the panel and lapped at my arm. I told my co-pilot, "Take control of the aircraft!" while I grabbed the fire extinguisher and smothered the flames with foam. I then began pulling circuit breakers to cut off the electricity to that panel.

After taking back the controls, I made an emergency landing at a nearby secure base. Fortunately, my Nomex flight suit protected me from getting burned.

Three weeks before I was to head home and be discharged from the Army, I was on the flight line inspecting my aircraft when a battalion officer came up to me and said, "Mr. Miller, battalion has been authorized to promote you to first lieutenant." The catch was—I had learned there's always a catch—I would need to agree to extend my tour for another six months.

I figured that I had just about maxed out my good luck by then and declined the promotion.

A couple of days later, my company commander called me into his office and said, "Our company is currently at capacity with pilots. I've decided to take you off flying status and have you work in the operations center until you leave country."

"Why?" I asked.

"I don't want to write your parents and tell them their son has been killed when you have only two weeks before you are due to be discharged from the Army. Besides, Dan, after serving a year and half flying armed attack helicopters in Vietnam, you have flown more missions than any one pilot I know."

I wasn't all that happy with his decision but had no choice in the matter. So, my combat mission flying ended two weeks before I left Vietnam.

On November 16, 1969, I boarded a commercial Boeing 707 on my way to Travis Air Force Base in California. From Travis, I was bussed to Oakland where I was processed through and received an honorable discharge from the Army. I was also awarded an additional eleven air medals for the combat missions I had flown as a Cobra pilot. That made a total of forty-four air medals.

During my year and half of duty in Vietnam, I had flown 1,382 combat hours and over 500 combat missions, which included over 240 night hours. My helicopters had been hit with numerous bullets, sometimes hitting vital parts of my helicopter where I had to make emergency landings. I had dozens of close calls, including my tail rotor failure and two emergency landings in a Cobra, yet I was never wounded. My guardian angel had definitely been working overtime while watching over me.

My parents drove down from Lake Almanor to pick me up, about a five-hour drive. I was now a civilian again which would entail a long process of readjustment. Again, I didn't realize what effect all the combat missions I had flown would have on me then and in the future.

✈ THIRTEEN ✈

My East Coast Girl

WHEN I ARRIVED AT MY parent's house on Lake Almanor, there was six feet of snow on the ground with an outside temperature of twenty degrees. Going from the hot, humid weather at sea level to the snowy cold at the 4,500 feet elevation of the Sierra Mountains was quite an adjustment for me.

In Vietnam, I became use to the sound of mortars, machine gun fire, and 105-Howitzers being fired during the day and night. Now, the deep snow covering the ground created a muffled silence. This resulted in many restless and sleepless nights. At times, I'd wake up in a cold sweat. Before going into the Army, I loved living in the mountains and the quietness of the country, but now I had to leave this serenity. I had to go to where there was some excitement and noise.

John, my good friend, had been stationed at Fort Walters, Texas, as a flight instructor while I was in Germany and Vietnam. That's where he met and dated Darenda who had been born and raised in Texas. They were married while he was stationed at Fort Walters. John and Darenda moved to Sacramento after he was discharged from the army.

One day in February of 1970, I packed up my things, took a bus to Sacramento and moved in with John and Darenda.

A few days later, I took a bus to San Francisco where I picked up my new 1970 gold Chevy Malibu Super Sport that I had ordered through the PX when I was stationed in Germany.

Opening day of fishing season, John and I drove to Lake Almanor and stayed at my mom and dad's house in Prattville.

Early Saturday morning, we headed for the stream Dad had told me about. The drive took about forty-five minutes up an old logging road. It was cold, and there was a good amount of snow still on the ground because we were now at an elevation of 5,500 feet.

John, as usual, began fishing ahead of me. I'm a methodical fisherman, so I took my time as I worked my way downstream. I hit every area on the stream I thought would be a good place for a trout to lie. As I let my line drift behind a small log that was partially in the water and began slowly reeling in my line, it became taut. I was thinking I had caught my hook on the log. As I began putting more pressure on the line, my pole bent over, nearly jerking it out of my cold hands. After about a five-minute battle, I landed a five-pound rainbow trout.

All I wanted to do was to find John and show him my prize and gloat a little . . . well, maybe more than a little. We had been very competitive since the day we met, in a friendly sort of way, of course.

I stuffed the trout in my creel and began fishing faster than usual. I continued to work my way downstream hoping to catch up with John. When I saw some brush overhanging the bank, I began letting my line drift under it. A trout hit my bait hard and after several minutes of fighting the fish, I landed a four-pound rainbow. Since my small creel wouldn't hold the two fish, I found a stick to string the fish on.

I tried to suppress my ear-to-ear grin when I finally came upon John sitting on a log with parts of his reel spread on top of a large rock. He couldn't believe the size of my two fish as he hadn't had a bite up to that point. John was in a panic because just before I got to where he was fishing, his reel had broken. With much difficulty, he had jerry-rigged his reel so he could fish. By the time we got back to the house, we had caught two four- and two five-pound rainbows.

Dad's younger sister Ruth and her husband had purchased a 300-year old house on Cape Cod, Massachusetts. Aunt Ruth came out to California to have Christmas with us that December and to spend some time with her family. While there, she asked if I would be willing to come to Cape Cod the following summer and work on her house that needed some repairs. Not having any other plans and since I wouldn't be going back to college until September, I agreed. In June of 1970, I drove from Sacramento to Cape Cod.

Aunt Ruth had given me directions to her house, but she left out some important details. Driving onto the Cape, I found what I thought was the off-ramp to her house, but I turned left instead of right, a detail her directions lacked. After about a mile, I came to an old village store appropriately named, "The Old Village Store."

I walked into the store where an older woman and a younger woman stood behind the counter. "Can you give me directions to the Sampson house?" I asked. Then I asked for a pack of cigarettes. I noticed the glance that passed between the two women when I asked for the cigarettes. It was even stranger when the older woman said, "Oh, you smoke."

I didn't know it but my aunt and the owner of the store had "conspired" to have their youngest daughter take me to the beach one day. The lady behind the counter had figured out who I was because of the California license plates on my car and my asking directions to the Sampson place.

I quickly found what would be my home for the summer. Aunt Ruth was Dad's baby sister and, shall I say, was very outgoing. She had been a princess in the Pasadena Rose Bowl Parade, been a B movie actor and had been, up to that point, married to five different men.

A couple of days after arriving, she informed me that she had asked the owner of the village store if her youngest daughter would take me to the beach. "Her name is Priscilla, and she'll be picking you up in about an hour." I wasn't at all happy about this arrangement until Priscilla arrived. She was wearing a bikini, had long red hair, and was very attractive. *This might turn out well after all*, I thought.

Priscilla and I hit it off right from the start as she drove me to a local beach named Sandy Neck. Even though it was summer, the water of the Atlantic Ocean was cold. Priscilla said, "You will never get in unless you just run into the water and dive in." To demonstrate, she ran into the water and dove in. She stood up, turned around to face me, waved her arm, and said, "Come on in, the water's great."

The water was so cold she didn't realize her bikini top had slipped down when she dove into the water.

I may have paused a second or two more than I should have, but being a gentleman, I said, "You might want to adjust your top," which she quickly did. (Priscilla has reluctantly given me permission to share that revealing bit of my story.)

After swimming, as we were lying on the beach enjoying the sun, I began reciting the poem, "The Cremation of Sam McGee" by Robert Service. That probably wasn't the most romantic poem I could have chosen for our first date, but she listened anyway.

I had been expecting a stuffy East Coast girl who did everything properly, but Priscilla turned out to be funny and witty and very intelligent. As we talked that afternoon, we discovered we had a lot in common.

From that time on and for the whole summer, we saw each other whenever we could arrange it. We had to get creative with me working at my aunt's and Priscilla working two jobs. Our dates usually included lunch at a local café as well as meeting again around 11:00 or 12:00 at night at the private night club where she was a waitress.

Priscilla had captured my heart. She had a great sense of humor, and it seemed as if we were constantly laughing at one thing or another. She showed me many historical sites in the area that I had read about in history books.

The end of August was nearing, and with it came time for me to leave as college would be starting the first week in September. After giving it much thought, I knew I loved Priscilla and wanted to ask her to marry me. I had Aunt Ruth's current husband, Marvin, drive me to a local jewelry store where I purchased an engagement ring.

A couple of days before I was due to drive back to California, I had arranged to meet Priscilla around midnight behind the club where she was a waitress. When she could finally take a break, she came out the back of the club, and I brought out the ring and proposed to her right next to the garbage cans. Amazingly, she accepted. I'm actually a romantic at heart, but my choice of a place to propose wasn't exactly evidence of that.

After we said our good-byes the following day, I drove from Cape Cod to Sacramento in three days. The stretch from Omaha, Nebraska to Sacramento I did in twenty-three hours. I averaged around one hundred miles an hour from Salt Lake City to Reno Nevada. Once, another car even passed me.

In Sacramento, John told me the California National Guard was looking for pilots, so after some investigation, both of us joined the guard as helicopter pilots. At that time, we were the most experienced pilots in our guard unit. The part-time pay was good and we could maintain our flight status. Since I had already met my full-time military commitments, I could quit the guard at any time by giving them ninety days written notice. This proved to be important a few years later. I was also required to attend two weeks of summer camp each year.

During my six-year stint in the guard, I was a flight instructor for the Ch-34 and the UH-B, D and H helicopters. I was also qualified in the OH-58 Bell Jet Ranger.

Before I left Cape Cod, I had registered for college and began classes the first week in September, giving me a monthly stipend from the government on the GI Bill.

On December 23, 1970, I flew to Boston where Priscilla's younger brother Jonathan met me at the airport. He drove me to the Cape where I stayed with Aunt Ruth and her husband. My parents along with my sister Julie and her husband Justin flew out the next day to join us.

My wild bachelor party consisted of her two brothers, one of whom I had just met that day, taking me to a local pub where each of us had one drink then went home. The conversation wasn't very stimulating as I recall. It seemed to be an awkward time for all three of us.

On December 27, 1970, we were married in the West Parish Church in West Barnstable, Massachusetts, the church Priscilla had attended growing up, one of the oldest churches in the United States as it was built in 1717. Dad was my best man.

After the wedding, Priscilla and I honeymooned in Phoenix, Arizona before settling in Sacramento, California. During the first year of our marriage, I was still going to school and Priscilla worked in Governor Reagan's office. We enjoyed doing things together, day trips on the weekends, trips to my parents' house on Lake Almanor, and board games in the evenings. In the summers we would waterski, swim, and fish, and in the winters, we'd ski and go toboggan sledding. It was a wonderful time of love and laughter, but that would soon change.

The first weekend in May of 1971 was the opening of fishing season. John, Darenda, Priscilla, and I drove up to Lake Almanor where we spent the weekend with my parents. There was still some snow on the ground and the nighttime outside temperatures dropped down into the teens.

Saturday morning at 5:00 a.m., John and I headed for our favorite fishing stream. We drove along a logging road for about forty-five minutes until we arrived at the upper part of the stream where we planned to start fishing. We were at a higher elevation than the house. Snow overhung the stream banks and icicles hung down from the trees into the stream.

As soon as we could see, we began fishing. I was wearing thermal underwear, heavy woolen socks, gloves, a heavy coat and hat, and had a hand warmer and survival kit.

John began fishing ahead of me, and I soon lost sight of him. As soon as I could, I crossed over to the other side of the stream because there wasn't as much brush and as many trees on that side of the stream.

I had been fishing for about ten minutes when I stepped up onto a snowbank that was overhanging the stream by about eight feet. Suddenly, the snowbank gave way, and I fell toward the stream. On my way down, my right foot became caught in the roots of a fallen tree, causing my leg to twist and my right kneecap to pop out of place and lodge against my knee joint.

I was in the freezing water and in a great deal of pain. I knew I had to get out of the water and fast. Despite the excruciating pain in my leg, I climbed up onto a tree stump that was next to the stream. I looked down at my leg and saw it was locked in a painful and odd angle.

Standing on my good leg, I threw my fishing rod and other gear up onto the bank above and out of the way. I began clawing away at the snow bank until I could pull myself up and onto the bank above. All this time, I hollered for John, but he was too far downstream to hear me.

By now my clothes were covered with ice, my leg was beginning to cramp up, and I could barely move. I knew from my survival training that I couldn't allow myself to fall asleep, so after about an hour of lying on the snow when I began to feel drowsy, I began singing and telling myself stories out loud, doing whatever I could think of to keep awake.

I had been lying there for about two hours when I heard a pickup truck coming down the logging road about a hundred yards away. I began yelling as loud as I could, "Help! Help!" I knew I was in serious trouble and about to pass out.

I didn't know it at the time, but the person coming down the road was Uncle Paul, my dad's youngest brother along with his friend Gobble. Before leaving Sacramento, I had told Uncle Paul where we would be fishing but didn't think he would be coming up. They had left Sacramento at 3:00 a.m. that morning and were now driving down the logging road toward the stream.

Their car heater was on high, the windows were up, and they were talking when Gobble said, "I think I heard someone yelling for help." When Uncle Paul stopped the pickup and rolled down the window, they both heard me yelling. Uncle Paul said to Gobble, "That sounds like Danny."

It took the two of them about ten minutes to get to the stream because there was a marsh between where I was and the road. To complicate matters, I was on the other side of the stream. Fortunately, there was a large tree lying across the stream connecting the top of the two banks.

Gobble started hiking downstream to find John while Uncle Paul began constructing a litter using some fallen limbs he found on the ground and a rope he had in his truck. About twenty minutes later, Gobble came back with John.

Because I was in so much pain, there was no way I was going to let them drag me across on that fallen tree, I needed to do this "my way."

John inched his way over on the ice-covered log and tied a rope to a tree on my side. After retrieving my rod and gear, he worked his way back to the other side where Uncle Paul secured the rope to another tree.

Now came the hard part. I slowly worked my way up on to the log, and holding onto the rope began pulling and inching my way across the stream. There were several tree limbs in my way and maneuvering around them was difficult with my useless leg. It took me about twenty minutes to go thirty feet.

When I finally got to the other side, they placed me on the litter Uncle Paul had made and carried me to the road. Meanwhile, John had gone to get the pickup.

Since there was nothing else Uncle Paul and Gobble could do, they decided to stay and take advantage of the fishing while John drove me to the hospital in Chester about forty minutes away.

I was cold and covered with ice so John gave me the pint of blackberry brandy he had brought along in his survival kit. As we drove to the hospital, I began drinking the brandy. Between the truck heater putting out heat like a blast furnace and the blackberry brandy, I was feeling no pain by the time we reached the hospital.

The hospital staff thought I had gotten drunk and fallen into the stream so they weren't too sympathetic to my condition until John finally explained, with a sheepish grin, what had really happened.

As hard as the doctor tried, he couldn't pop my kneecap back in place so said he needed to do it surgically. But the anesthesiologist had to wait until I sobered up before putting me under. The decision was made to keep me overnight and operate in the morning.

The next morning, I was sober and feeling pain again. The doctor tried one last time to pop my kneecap back into place by hand, and this time it worked. They bandaged my swollen knee and gave me some crutches and pain pills. I left the hospital ready to do some more fishing, much to Priscilla's disgust.

It's hard for me to write about the early years of our marriage because I realize how often I was emotionally and physically absent from my family. The two passions of my life were flying and gambling. I won't try to describe what those years were like from Priscilla's perspective.

All I can say is that I am so grateful that our marriage survived in spite of my destructive behaviors.

Priscilla feels God took her stubborn refusal to consider divorce and her prideful determination to "fix" me and used them for His own purposes. He certainly had to humble us both over that six-year period.

During the years to come, I began gambling at local card rooms. This became such a regular occurrence to the point that I was fixated on being the best card player I could be. I was consumed with this passion and would practice shuffling, manipulating, and memorizing card orders four to five hours a day. I often did this on our dining room table. The constant sound of the plastic cards hitting against the Formica table caused Priscilla to spend most of that time outside or in another room. Our relationship was deteriorating at a rapid rate.

Maintaining flying status in the guard required pilots to fly a certain number of day and night hours each year. John and I found creative ways to do this.

When the San Francisco 49ers or Oakland Raiders played a Monday night football game, television stations blacked out transmission of the games for one hundred miles. This meant Sacramento would not receive the game. On those Monday nights, John and I often reserved a helicopter to get in some of our flight time. We would then fly up to our hometown of Willows, which is about ninety miles north of Sacramento, and watch part of the game with some friends at the local pizza parlor.

On December 19, 1971, I had reserved a CH-34 helicopter and John and I and a crew chief flew up to Willows and spent a couple of hours watching the football game. On our return flight to Mather Air Force Base, I was at the controls. We were about five miles north of Sacramento, flying at an altitude of 2,000 feet, when I heard a loud bang and the engine completely quit running. I immediately put the helicopter into an autorotation mode, which meant we were falling like a rock. I began looking for a place to land and at the same time calling a Mayday to the local airfields and control center.

We were over flooded rice fields that wouldn't have been safe to land in because of the soft ground. Besides, we would have gotten our feet wet, and I had just polished my boots that afternoon.

As we were falling to the ground, John spotted a narrow dirt road that ran between two rice paddies. In the dark, I lined the helicopter up to land on the road, went through the emergency landing procedures, very quickly leveled off, and creased the three wheels down onto the middle of the dirt road sweet as you please. We landed without a scratch.

After turning off all electrical, fuel, and other systems, we got out and saw that the two front tires were overhanging each side of the road with no room to spare. I found out later there had been a mechanical failure of one of the engine components. I was given a commendation medal for landing the helicopter safely.

In March of 1972, our daughter Jessica was born. I wanted to have a family, which included children but not the responsibility. Even though I was married, I loved my independence. It wasn't until Jessica was three or four that I felt somewhat engaged in her life. I truly believe that, even though I was somewhat reckless and adventurous in my early years, I would have settled down eventually and been a good husband and parent. I had a great role model in my parents, but the many life and death situations I found myself in so many times during my tours in Vietnam really messed me up emotionally.

During this time, we got our registered black Labrador retriever puppy, Maximus Major. When Max grew up, he weighed ninety-five pounds. I spent very little time training Max, yet he turned out to be a fantastic bird dog, excellent at retrieving ducks. Max was very protective of Jessica and would follow her all around the house and yard. She loved playing in the mud with Max; she took after her dad in that regard.

⛨ FOURTEEN ⛨

A Gambling Man

EACH SUMMER OUR HELICOPTER UNIT was required to spend two weeks of summer camp at Camp Roberts, located near the town of Paso Robles, in the middle of the state near the Pacific coast. During the summer camp of 1972, my primary crew chief was the cousin of Wayne Rogers who starred in the TV series, *M*A*S*H*. Wayne Rogers owned a ranch near Paso Robles, and my crew chief had arranged for me to have dinner with Wayne and his wife. Before dinner, the three of us went rabbit hunting on his ranch. We had a great time riding around in his jeep, shooting rabbits and rats. Wayne's wife was an excellent cook, and I enjoyed getting to know him as well as sharing several adventure stories with each other.

While at summer camp, I trained one of our newer pilots, a captain, how to fly the CH-34. While we were practicing "touch and goes," I thought I'd add a little excitement to our training. As he began lining up the helicopter with the runway to make a steep approach, I cut the engine so he could practice an autorotation.

When I cut the engine, the pilot froze.

We were headed for the ground. He had such a vise grip on the controls that I couldn't do anything. I screamed at him, "Release the controls!" Finally, I hit him as hard as I could on the side of his helmet. This brought him out of the state he was in, and he released the controls.

I landed the helicopter with only seconds to spare before we would have crashed. He desperately wanted to get out, but I wasn't about to let him out. I flew us back up and around, lined us up with the airstrip, then had him get "lightly" on the controls with me as I did two more autorotations. Seeing the sweat rolling down his face, I had pity on him and called it a day.

We moved to Folsom, California, where I enrolled at Sacramento State that fall. I spent the next year and half going to school on the GI Bill and flying helicopters for the guard. In January of 1974, I graduated with a bachelor of science degree in business administration.

For the next few months, I didn't do much. As usual, I was restless but didn't know what I wanted to do for a living. I didn't put a lot of effort into finding a job, which caused a great deal of stress on our young marriage. Sometimes I would spend hours just playing with Jessica.

Priscilla was still working in Governor Reagan's mail room, and one of her duties each day was to deliver his mail to him. Since she was fluent in French, she also had occasions to be an interpreter when French-speaking dignitaries visited the state capital.

In June of 1974, I took a summer job flying helicopters out of Fort Erwin located north of Barstow, California, about fifteen miles west of Death Valley. The average daytime temperatures would reach 110 degrees. One day, the temperature reached a scorching 121 degrees, and the helicopters I flew did not have air conditioning. My primary responsibility was flying people and supplies to different locations around the Mojave Desert.

One day, I was asked to fly to the Burbank airport near Los Angeles. I was to pick up some dignitaries and fly them to the Marine base at

Barstow the next morning. My co-pilot was from LA so that night he took me to a local nightclub. He said this club was often frequented by movie stars. I don't remember seeing any movie stars that night, but the club had a great band and the food was great. It was a nice change from the mess hall food I had been eating. The next morning, we picked up our passengers and after dropping them off at the Marine base, we returned to Fort Erwin.

While flying for the guard that August, I was asked to fly a search and rescue mission in the Sierra Mountains to look for a boy who had gotten lost at a Boy Scout camp. The camp was located at an elevation of 6,500 feet. The only helicopter available was a CH-34 which was not my first choice for a search and rescue helicopter. John happened to be available, so the two of us, along with our crew chief and a medic from the Air Force, took off for the search area.

When we reached the search area, I called the people on the ground and asked for instructions. I was asked to set down in a small clearing not much larger than our helicopter, which I did. John manned the controls, as I didn't shut down, while I walked over to the search and rescue team and they showed me on the map the area I was to concentrate on.

After getting back in the helicopter, I took back the controls and went through the normal pre-takeoff checks. I began pulling in power as I lifted out of the landing area. At about a hundred feet above the ground, the helicopter experienced a sudden partial engine failure. We crashed into several trees and landed hard on the ground. Fortunately, none of us was injured, but the helicopter sustained major damage to the fuselage and all four rotor blades.

I was always looking for things to do or places to go, which seldom included Priscilla. It was strange, we had great times when we visited my parents' house, but when back in our own home, all I wanted to do was go off and do something by myself.

Late in August, one of the officers who worked full time for the California guard and owned a large boat, invited John and me fishing on the Sacramento River just south of Sacramento. We had been fishing for a couple of hours and hadn't caught anything so we anchored near the bank of the river and let our lines drift out the back of the boat.

We had been playing cards and drinking beer for about an hour when my pole slowly began to bend over. I started to pull on my line thinking a log had rolled over my hook. My pole started to jerk, and I quickly realized I had a fish on my line. At one point, after fighting this fish for about two hours, the fish, a sturgeon, decided to surface.

By this time there were about two hundred people standing on the high levee banks of the river watching me fight this fish. It came about three quarters of the way out of the water making a huge wave as it fell back into the water. The people on the bank went crazy. A county sheriff who was watching with everyone else yelled, "Do you want to borrow my shotgun?" The crowd laughed.

I fought that sturgeon for about another hour until finally my line broke, and the fish was lost. Unfortunately, I only had twenty-five-pound test line on my reel. I wasn't expecting to hook such a large fish.

My arms felt like rubber, and I was exhausted but thrilled. On our way home, we stopped at a local bar near where we had been fishing. Several fishermen in the bar had been watching me fight that fish, and said they estimated the sturgeon weighed up to 300 pounds and was about nine feet in length.

Because of dad's friendship with one of the vice presidents of PG&E, I was enrolled into the company's management training program. This was a select group of trainees who, in the company's view, would become the company's top management in the future. I only lasted there six months.

Instead, by February of 1975, I became a professional gambler. This new profession became the primary focus of my life. Besides cards, my betting included sports games, the weather, or even who could spit the farthest.

Priscilla was disgusted and afraid. An even greater rift formed between Priscilla and me that resulted in many anxious, tearful, and sleepless nights for her.

I didn't know why I had to keep pushing the edge. I needed to be challenged in my life and gambling seemed to satisfy part of that urge.

Our relationship was falling apart at a rapid rate. Sometimes I would take off and go fishing or gambling someplace for several days and not even tell her where I was going or when I would be back.

Even though I enjoyed being with our daughter, Jessica, I was feeling constrained. I wanted the freedom to do whatever I wanted and not be burdened with the responsibility of a family. Much of this thinking I kept to myself, but Priscilla sensed my unhappiness.

I played a card game called Low Ball. My day would often begin around 4:00 or 5:00 in the afternoon, and I'd return home at 2:00 or 3:00 in the morning. For a while, I was very successful at it, but it was a sleazy way of making a living. I played in smoke-filled cardrooms where I had access to just about any kind of illegal activity or drug you could think of. Fortunately, I had no desire to take drugs or drink alcohol.

We owned a nice house on third of an acre of land just outside of Sacramento. On the property were several fruit trees, a stream running through it, and a large garden. We still had the two acres of land in Hawaii I had purchased while in Vietnam, a new car, a pickup, expensive clothes, and other possessions.

I became such a good card player that I gained the reputation for being someone other gamblers wanted to play against in those smoke-filled card rooms. When I played, I had no mercy on the people I played with. So other players wanted to take me down a notch or two by beating me.

Because I didn't care who I hurt, I was constantly aware that I might cross the wrong person at any time, so I carried a loaded shotgun and sometimes a pistol in my pickup wherever I went.

One night or early morning as I was heading home, I saw the flashing lights of a Sacramento police car behind and a voice on the loud speaker ordered me to pull over. The officer came up to my window leaned down and said, "Don't move. Keep your hands on the steering wheel. You're wanted for murder."

Not comprehending why he was saying this, I said, "Officer, you've made a mistake. I haven't killed anyone."

"There is no mistake, you low life scum. You're going to jail for the rest of your life."

I was getting suspicious by then. If I was wanted for murder, why hadn't he pulled his pistol and ordered me out of my truck? Then I heard some giggling and tapping on the passenger side window. As I turned to see what was going on, there was my good friend Bert, a Sacramento police officer, making faces at me through the window and laughing. He was also a helicopter pilot with the guard, and we often flew together. Bert and I would ride our motorcycles together, me on my 750 Honda Super Sport motorcycle and Bert on his Harley.

In July of 1975, Priscilla found she was pregnant again. Even though Priscilla loved being a mother, she was terrified at what this would do to our fragile and deteriorating relationship. She felt hopeless and often had suicidal thoughts.

For me, this was not a pleasant announcement. I wanted more freedom and another child would constrain my freedom even more.

The love I had for Priscilla when we were first married, had turned to irritation and dissatisfaction.

At times when I didn't feel like risking my own money, I would shill for the owners of various card rooms, which provided me with a take of the table winnings. My arrogance and status among the other card players began to be my ruin, however. My gambling soon got excessive, and I began losing everything I owned.

I began taking chances I shouldn't have, and my winning streak ended. I had to begin selling our possessions. Not being able to pay bills became a regular occurrence. Despite our indebtedness, I always carried enough money with me to get into a card game when I had the chance.

⬛ FIFTEEN ⬛

A Pivotal Moment

OUR SON JIM WAS BORN in April of 1976. Again, as with Jessica, I wasn't in a good frame of mind to welcome a son into the world; I was too consumed with my own life. I wanted a family, but I did everything opposite of what a good father should do. Our life together was a mess, and my lifestyle hurt everyone.

By now, our utilities had been shut off, and creditors began calling at all times during the day and night. Often, I wouldn't be home, and Priscilla had to handle these calls, which were, at times, threatening.

Desperate to find relief, Priscilla packed her bags and flew to Massachusetts with four-year-old Jessica and our son Jim, only two months old. She said, "I want to show off our new baby and Jessica to everyone."

What was intended to be a short visit, turned out to be a five-month separation with Priscilla taking a waitressing job to help pay for our house mortgage.

I was sorry they were gone, yet at the same time, felt relieved from my responsibilities. My newfound independence now resulted in me doing things and going places I would not have done before our separation.

I gave my ninety-day notice to the California National Guard and quit flying. My life was so messed up at this point that I walked away from the most enjoyable and rewarding part of my life, flying helicopters.

By the end of September 1976, I had lost everything we owned due to my gambling. I sold our home, the land in Hawaii, the pickup, the motorcycle, everything of value including a valuable coin collection Priscilla's dad had given to her. I was thousands of dollars in debt with about ten creditors after me. My credit was overextended in six card rooms, my bank, and a credit card company.

But I refused to ask my parents for financial help. I could not bring myself to involve them in my troubles; I loved them too much to do so.

I just need a break, I thought. I was still thinking I could turn my bad luck around by my own strength and smarts.

One morning in early October, I woke up and remembered a letter my Aunt Margaret, Dad's older sister, had written me. I remembered the letter had come in a blue envelope. Searching everywhere for that letter, I finally found it at the bottom of a file drawer filled with many unopened bills. It was a mystery to me at the time why I had kept that letter and why I had such an intense drive to find it. Normally I would have just thrown it away unopened.

Aunt Margaret's letter invited me to come live with her and her family in their house on Mercer Island, Washington. A few days after reading Margaret's letter, my wild, penniless lifestyle came to a halt. A so-called friend of mine, a fellow gambler, told me someone I had crossed was putting out a warrant for my arrest.

I knew I had to get out of town and fast. All my options had run out. I told my mom and dad what I was planning to do, but not why. A few days later they drove down with a truck to help pack up what meager possessions Priscilla and I had left and move them to our family cabin near Lake Almanor.

After spending a few days with my parents, I packed our Mazda station wagon (I had sold my Malibu) with whatever I really needed and drove to Mercer Island to live with Dad's older sister Margaret and her husband George.

The next month and half would turn out to be one of the most humiliating and desperate times of my life. I was now dependent on someone else to help me through my difficulties. I had never really acknowledged I needed help before. Priscilla and the children were still in Massachusetts.

The first Sunday I was in their home, Margaret asked me to go to church with them. This was the last thing I wanted to do but felt obligated because I was living in their house. During the service, there was a time for those in attendance to stand up and share a prayer request or praise or introduce a guest.

Uncle George, who was in the choir, stood up and said to the entire congregation, "Margaret and I are pleased to announce that our nephew, Dan Miller, Margaret's brother's son, has come to live with us for a while."

I was furious. *How could he embarrass me in front of all his friends that way?* My aunt, who I had been sitting next to said later that during that service she could see me shaking with rage and felt a cold chill coming off me—I was *that* angry. I didn't go back to church with them again.

Despite my attitude, George gave me work in his business. I soon grew to dislike him because I was now dependent on his kindness. He was always talking to me about religious things, and I didn't want to hear it.

I had always counted on my ability to make people believe what I wanted them to believe. After some convincing persuasion on my part, Margaret called Priscilla and talked her into to coming to Washington. Margaret was convinced I wanted to start a new life with my family. About a week later, Priscilla, along with four-year-old Jessica and seven-month-old Jimmy, packed their bags and flew to Seattle.

It wasn't long before our life together in the unfinished basement of my aunt's house became strained again. Our relationship was being lived out in virtual silence. Priscilla and the kids spent most of their time upstairs with people she barely knew.

When I wasn't working for my uncle, I went on job interviews, but there weren't a lot of options to choose from. I was becoming more and more angry and withdrawn. All I wanted to do was to get a stake and begin playing cards again. Given a break, I knew I could turn my bad luck streak around.

No matter with whom I interviewed, I was either over qualified or a company didn't have an opening with my qualifications. I joked that my resume´ should have read "College graduate with average grades, ex-helicopter pilot, and ex-professional gambler." I was becoming progressively angrier.

Tuesday afternoon, December 7, 1976, I went on a job interview with a battery company in Tukwila. The person doing the interview was up from their corporate offices in Portland, Oregon. At the conclusion of the interview the manager said, "Mr. Miller, I would like to hire you, but I don't have a position that would take advantage of your business administration degree."

I drove back to the house angry and bitter thinking, "Why is this happening to me?"

I was stretched out on the couch in my aunt's basement watching cartoons on the TV when Priscilla came downstairs. She said a professional football player, Norm Evans of the Seattle Seahawks, was speaking at the church that night. "Will you go with me?" she asked.

I said "No," which was odd because I would normally have jumped at a chance to meet a professional football player. I loved watching sports on TV and was in the habit of watching professional and college football all weekend long and knew the names of many of the players.

The second thing that was odd was Priscilla asking me to go with her to hear a football player. She hated football because of the hours I spent watching sports.

She was so determined to go, Priscilla persisted to the point of breaking down crying. Finally, my irritation got the best of me, and said I would go just to get her off my back. Defensive as I was, I felt she was constantly nagging and complaining. Actually, she did very little, but it was at a point in our relationship where I would react negatively to just about anything she said.

By saying yes to Priscilla, my life took a dramatic turn, never to be the same again.

We arrived at the church a few minutes before 7:00 p.m. Norm and his wife, Bobbie, were not there. The later it got, the madder I was becoming. As I was sitting there, I made up my mind that on the way home, I was going to tell Priscilla I wanted a divorce. By 7:20 p.m., I was about to get up and leave when Norm and Bobbie walked into the sanctuary where they were to speak. to the sixty or seventy people present.

When the audience began clapping for them, I thought, *What about me? I'm a highly- decorated helicopter pilot and a respected professional gambler.* That was the self-centered frame of mind I was in.

After the introduction by Bud Palmberg, the senior pastor, and before they began to speak, Norm turned to his wife Bobbie. In front of everyone present he said, "Bobbie, please forgive me for getting upset with you on the way over here." He then told those present that the reason they were late was because Bobbie had forgotten to bring the directions to the church, and he had gotten upset with her. I couldn't believe my ears. How in the world could this professional football player with two Super Bowl rings to his credit do such a lowly thing as apologize to his wife in front of all those stupid people?

They began their presentation by putting on aprons and acting as if they were in a kitchen speaking about how God works in their marriage.

Before a minute or two had passed, a curious thing happened to me. What felt like a light, gray veil was placed over my eyes and my ears were blocked from hearing anything that was being said in the room. I then became aware of every bad thing I had ever done in my life. I saw every circumstance all at the same time and yet, it was as if I was seeing each one separately. Even today I can't fully describe what I was experiencing.

It was extremely clear to me that I had done all these things against God. I was devastated. Faced with this terrifying realization but not really knowing anything about God, I internally, cried out in great anguish, *God help me. Please help me.*

Instantly, all the hate, anger, and bitterness within me disappeared. I could feel everything within me being changed. At that very instant, my eyes and ears cleared and I heard Norm say, "If anyone would like to receive Jesus Christ into their heart please pray with me," and I did. Forty-five minutes had passed from the time Norm and Bobbie began speaking up to this point.

As soon as I prayed that prayer, a non-verbal voice inside said to me, *You need to tell someone.*

Who? I knew without any doubt that God had done something to me, but I didn't understand any of it. Then the voice came into my head again, *You need to tell someone.* Not knowing what to do or understanding what was going on inside of me, I got up quickly and walked to the back of the sanctuary and sat down at a desk in the library. I proceeded to fill out an information card Norm had passed out to everyone and handed it to one of the ushers.

While I can't remember anything Norm and Bobbie said or did during those forty-five minutes, Priscilla heard every word. She did not know at the time why she had pushed so hard to get me to attend this event. Her fear of my hair-trigger anger toward her usually made her avoid any confrontation with me. This was especially true since we were living in my aunt and uncle's home. It was fine with her that we sat on the church pew with some distance between us.

She heard Norm and Bobbie share about struggles in their relationship using honest accounts of their failings, sprinkled with lots of humor and forgiveness. It was like a glimpse of light after six years of our increasingly dark marriage.

When they offered an invitation to pray a prayer of salvation, she had become so aware of her exhaustion from years of trying to make things work in her own strength, that she poured out her anguish to Jesus and asked Him to take over her life. She immediately felt the truth of those beautiful words from Matthew, "Come to Me, you who are weary and heavy-laden, and I will give you rest" (Matt. 7:28). She felt a lightness of spirit and knew God had changed her life.

Priscilla was experiencing such a wonderful closeness with God that she hadn't even been thinking about me. It was therefore a rude awakening when she saw me bolting from the pew to go the back of the church. She wrongly interpreted this as my desire to leave as quickly as possible because I was furious at her for insisting I come to church.

Reality came crashing back into her thoughts and she knew she would have to drive home with me and resume life in the basement of my aunt and uncle's home. She was certain of one thing from all that went on that evening, she was determined not to share with me how Jesus had changed her life with that prayer. There was no way she was going to allow me to trample on that holy moment with my scorn. We drove home and went to bed together in silence.

SIXTEEN

The Still, Small Voice

WEDNESDAY MORNING AT 9 A.M., I was still in my T-shirt and shorts when the phone rang. It was the manager of the battery company I had interviewed with the day before. He said he had talked with the district manager of a company that manufactured facsimile machines. If I could be at their office in Bellevue by 10:00 a.m., he would grant me an interview.

I put my military training to use as I quickly showered, shaved, put on my suit and was out the door in twenty minutes. The interview went well but did not end with a job offer. Yet as I drove home, I felt a peace that I hadn't experienced before. I couldn't explain it, but I knew everything was going to be okay.

The next three days were uneventful with neither of us saying much to each other, but the normal tension between us was missing.

That week, Aunt Margaret had arranged for Pastor Bud Palmberg to take me to lunch. The purpose of the lunch was to share with me about the good news Jesus offers and His plan for my life. Pastor Bud picked me up and drove me to a local restaurant in Bellevue. We had barely sat down when I began telling him about my experience on Tuesday night.

Pastor Bud sat there with a look of complete shock on his face.

Pastor Bud told me sometime later that as he sat in the church that Tuesday night he had been thinking that Norm and Bobbie's corny marriage skit wearing aprons wasn't going to reach anyone. He didn't know that Priscilla and I were hanging on for dear life.

That night, Priscilla and I lay in bed silent. Pastor Bud knew what had happened to me that Tuesday night but Priscilla didn't. We hadn't said more than a few words to each other for the past three days.

Then the non-verbal voice came back into my head again and said, *You need to pray with your wife.*

I don't know how to pray, I answered inside.

I couldn't get away from it. Finally, I gave in, turned on my side facing her and said, "Priscilla, will you pray with me?"

She was speechless and looked at me as if I were trying to make fun of her. We finally shared with each other about what had happened to us that Tuesday night. I also shared what went on during my lunch with Pastor Bud. We didn't get much sleep that night, but we did pray together and ask God to help us understand what had happened to us.

Saturday morning around 6:30 a.m., Pastor Bud had arranged to pick me up and take me to a men's Bible study that met every Saturday morning in one of the member's homes. I went to the study carrying the Bible I had received when I went through my non-memorable confirmation class. I hadn't opened it since it was given to me and don't remember packing it when I left California. It was a mystery to me how I found it.

As I sat there in a circle with about twenty other men, the leader said, "Please open your Bibles to the book of Mark, chapter eight." I began thumbing through Genesis, Exodus, Numbers, etc., not knowing anything about who this Mark was. Without drawing attention to what he was doing, the man sitting next to me casually reached over and turned the pages of my Bible to the book of Mark. The Scriptures say one must become like a child to enter the kingdom of heaven, and I was an infant. I felt grateful for that man sitting next to me.

Sunday morning Priscilla and I wanted to go to church together. We still hadn't told my aunt and uncle about our experiences. I was in the shower when this persistent, non-verbal voice said, *You need to tell someone.*

Who? Just tell me, I responded. We were now on our way to church. I was beginning to feel that our life together would never be the same.

As I sat in the pew, taking in all that was around me, the voice came back in my head and said, *You need to tell someone.* Priscilla told me later that I was, "fidgeting as if I had ants in my pants."

The time came in the service for the congregation to share. I knew then without any doubt, that this is what that voice inside me was leading up to.

I don't remember standing up, but the next thing I knew, I was standing there sharing with the congregation about the experience Priscilla and I had that Tuesday night.

Pastor Bud, as a rule, encouraged people to keep their sharing to no more than a minute or two at the most. When I continued speaking beyond that, he told me later how he had begun to stand up and ask me to close and share more after the service but had felt a strong pressure on his chest. He sat down knowing the Lord did not want him to interfere.

At the conclusion of the service, about a dozen women as well as many other people came up and began hugging me, kissing me on the cheek, crying, and praising God. I wondered why all these people were making such a fuss over Priscilla and me.

When we got back to the house, Aunt Margaret told me that she and her women's Bible study, as well as many in the church, had been praying for me for over ten years. She said, "The more we prayed, the worse you got."

I am a true believer that God honors persistent prayers. I also know now that the non-verbal voice I kept hearing was, and is, the Holy Spirit of God. I am so grateful He was so persistent and didn't give up on me.

SEVENTEEN

A New Life

THE DISTRICT MANAGER I HAD interviewed with the day after our conversion called me back. He offered me a job as the only salesperson in a small office with two service technicians. Even though he hired me to start that day, he didn't come up to train me until the first week in January.

The district manager, now my boss, told me in one of our later conversations that he and the manager of the battery company had been staying in the same hotel. They happened to be sitting next to each other in the hotel bar the same night Priscilla and I were at the church. The man from the battery company told my boss about the interview he had had with me that day and that he should consider hiring me.

I have always been and continue to be amazed at how involved the Lord is in our daily lives. He continues to work in our lives in ways we may never be aware of.

One Sunday a few weeks later, Pastor Bud gave a sermon about the concept of tithing and being a cheerful giver and giving back to the Lord's work out of what He had given us.

We were thousands of dollars in debt. We had little more than the clothes on our backs, but we both felt a strong leading to begin tithing from our gross income.

In the following years, we never missed paying a bill. It took us about six years of skimping and saving, but we paid off every one of our debts, including all the gambling debts I had accumulated during those dark days of my life. Someone once criticized me for paying off those debts. He said, "How can you give money to those card room owners when it is the Lord who is now providing your finances?"

I am convinced the Lord was honored by me rectifying the wrongs I had done before turning my life over to Him. If I hadn't paid off those debts, it could have hindered my witness in the future. We have lived modestly for all of our Christian lives, but since then we have never felt we have missed out on anything.

For the first couple of months after our commitment to Christ, Priscilla still felt some resentment toward me and was struggling to deal with it. I had become somewhat of a celebrity in the church by now, but she wanted people to know how badly I had treated her. Then one morning she happened to be watching a Christian television program and the pastor said, "I have a word of encouragement for someone who is struggling with resentment. That word comes from Joel 2:25: 'Then I will make up to you for the years that the swarming locust has eaten.'" When she shared this with me, I was overwhelmed at the healing the Lord was doing in our lives.

Priscilla and I became regular attenders and then members of Mercer Island Covenant Church. We joined a small group Bible study that met in one of our member's home.

We both enrolled in Bible Study Fellowship, which helped us greatly grow in our faith and understanding of the Bible. Priscilla eventually became a discussion leader for many years in the women's Bible Study Fellowship class.

During the thirteen years I spent in the men's class, I was a discussion leader for five years, a substitute teaching leader for three years, and an area administrator for four years.

Our children were also transformed in their faith and felt safe and protected by us and the church as they learned about Jesus' love for them.

The Lord gave me a fresh new love for Priscilla as well as for Jessica and Jim. I wanted to be the loving, Christ-centered husband and father I hadn't been in the earlier years of our lives together.

Our lives had changed.

Three months after our commitment to Christ, we invited some new friends to dinner. After dinner, Priscilla brought out a game of rummy and the four of us began playing. When it finally came my turn to deal the cards, a regular deck of playing cards, I thought, *I'll just wow them with some fancy card shuffling.* Okay, I wanted to show off.

I took the deck and split it in two. My idea was to put half of the deck in each hand, face the ends towards each other with space between the two half decks, then riffle the cards towards each other, stacking the cards in a nice neat pile in front of me. However, as I let go of the cards, they flew everywhere: in Priscilla's lap, on the floor, and in front of our guests. Priscilla had a look of shock on her face because she knew how many hours a day I had practiced shuffling and manipulating a deck of cards.

I, too, was somewhat astounded but chocked it up to being rusty since I had not manipulated a deck of cards for a while. After sheepishly gathering up all the cards, again I split the deck in two and started to shuffle the way most people do. As I began to riffle the cards together, my hands started shaking and the cards again scattered on the table before me. My friend's wife said, "It's okay, Dan, if you don't know how to shuffle cards."

Priscilla and I had been praying that the Lord would take away my desire to gamble. He not only did that, but He took away my ability also. If He hadn't taken away my ability, as with that night, I would have been tempted to do card tricks for anyone who wanted to watch.

I am so grateful for what the Lord did for me that night. It was a true answer to prayer. Since then, I do not play any game that involves a deck of playing cards.

EIGHTEEN

Who, Me? Teach?

IT HAD BEEN NINE MONTHS since Priscilla and I made a commitment to live our lives in obedience to our Savior and Lord Jesus Christ. Our life as a couple and a family had been growing stronger and stronger due to the Lord's influence in our lives. The wonderful teaching of Pastor Bud also contributed to our growth.

With the new fall Sunday school classes beginning, Priscilla and I talked about attending one of the adult classes together.

On the first Sunday of September 1977, as we walked into the church, I turned to Priscilla and said, "I think that I would like to help out in one of the children's Sunday school classes." This was odd although it didn't seem so to me at the time. Priscilla didn't even question it even though we had decided to attend an adult class together.

Even stranger, I usually didn't enjoy being around other people's children. My idea of helping was to run errands for the teacher, pass out papers, and clean up, etc. I didn't envision having direct contact with the children.

I spotted someone I thought was a leader in the church and asked her, "Do you know of anyone who might need help in one of the children's

Sunday school classes?" She said she didn't but to ask the senior pastor's wife, Donna Palmberg. She directed me to an upstairs classroom at the back of a small kitchen.

As I approached the door, I could hear voices so I knocked. The door was quickly opened and Donna Palmberg exclaimed, "Oh, Dan!"

I then told her about my conversation with the woman downstairs. "Do you know of any teacher who could use some help?"

"Dan, you're an answer to prayer," Donna quickly said. "Will you take over this class for a few minutes? There are some things I need to do downstairs; I'll be back as soon as I can." She was talking a mile a minute giving me a few brief instructions, which I did not comprehend at all. I was still trying to process that I would have to take over the Sunday school class for her.

The next thing I knew, the door shut, she was gone, and I was left standing in front of a closed door dressed in my black three-piece suit. I knew in the back of my mind there were some human beings behind me, but the defense mechanisms in my brain had blocked out what kind they were. I also knew I couldn't keep standing there for the next hour.

Having little choice in the matter, I turned around and there sitting on the orange shag carpet in this eight- by ten-foot room also used for storage were about a dozen two- and three-year-olds staring up at me. I immediately said in my mind, *God, this is not good.*

When we lived in Fair Oaks, California, Priscilla took care of her friend's two boys during the day. The older boy was about the age of Jessica. Sometimes I would come home during the day and would stare at the older boy and try to make him cry with a mean stare. This became such a problem that Priscilla had to stop taking care of her friend's children. I did not like being around other people's children, however, I would never have thought of hurting any child physically.

Many years after becoming a Christian, I had the opportunity to meet with this now twenty-five-year-old young man. I confessed my mean stares and asked for his forgiveness. He had no recollection of what I was talking about. The Lord had healed him and forgiven me of the way I had treated him.

Meanwhile, back in the Sunday school room, I had no idea what to do next. At that moment, I would rather have been anywhere than in that room with those children. I looked around for a place to sit and discovered the chairs would accommodate only half of me, so I sat down on the edge of a low table facing the children.

They stared at me, and I stared at them. Remembering that I was the adult in the room and that I should begin some kind of dialog, I asked, "What do you want to do?" Thankfully, the Lord had compassion on me as one of the children said, "Let's play with puzzles."

Another said, "Let's color."

Then one of the children said, "Read us a story."

I said to myself, *Yes, I can do that, I know how to read.*

One of the boys brought me a book from the bookcase. I opened it and was relieved to see large print and pictures. I needed all the help I could get.

As I was about to begin reading, a little girl stood up and came toward me, stepping around and over a couple of the other children. She was a little taller than the other children, quite plain in appearance and simply dressed. She asked, "Can I sit on your lap?"

Before I could ask her to sit down, she had climbed up on my leg and put her head on my chest as God melted my heart. As I sat there reading with this little girl on my lap, I could feel the love of God warming my heart. I never saw that child again after that Sunday.

There are many blessings I could tell you about my time with those children. Donna Palmberg did not return that morning. As it turned out, I was in that classroom every Sunday morning for an hour and fifteen minutes from that September to the following June. I say I was in that class because I didn't feel like the teacher. I played games, colored, put puzzles together with the kids, brought snacks, and read to them each Sunday, but it was the Lord who taught us.

As I read those Bible stories, I was reading them for the first time myself. I read about David, Peter, Paul, Ruth, Abraham, and especially the life of Jesus. I had no experience teaching a Sunday school class; what I had was a willing heart, and God did the rest.

Over the next several years, Priscilla and I taught every age group from those two- and three-year-olds through the sixth grade, and my love of children grew. The Lord took the dislike I had had for other people's children and replaced it with a special love in my heart for them.

I'm also grateful for how the Lord used Donna Palmberg in this process and her faithfulness to His leading. This has been one of the most memorable and gratifying experiences of my life, and I have had many.

☰ NINETEEN ☱

Learning to Serve

AS I WAS GROWING SPIRITUALLY, God was helping me in my new career as a businessman. For four years I worked for the company that first hired me.

During that time, two major events took place in our lives. In 1978, we were able to trade in our Mazda for a brown Toyota station wagon. I had a steady job but no credit. How we qualified for a loan was all the Lord's doing. That station wagon not only served as my business vehicle, we used it a lot for family outings.

Camping was one of our favorite adventures. We had this tent that was nine feet square and the center was about seven feet high so I could actually stand up in it. It weighed a ton and some of the fourteen steel poles that held it up were six feet in length. When we went camping with all our gear and supplies, there was barely enough room for us in the vehicle. With the car packed, I couldn't see out the back window so Jessica and Jim were my rearview mirrors. Jessica and Jim sat on our flattened out sleeping bags, hand-me-downs from my parents that would keep you warm if the temperature didn't drop below fifty degrees. If we would have gotten into a roll-over accident, none of us would have been hurt because we were packed in like sardines. I will say those camping trips were a hoot. The kids loved playing games and sleeping in that tent especially when it rained.

Another amazing provision for our family happened with the help of Aunt Margaret who was a real estate agent. The Lord provided a way for us to purchase a three-bedroom, 1,100-square-foot condo in the Newport Hills Townhomes that would be our home for the next seventeen years. This was made possible by the Lord because we had no money for a down payment and my credit was poor at best.

In 1980, I was laid off but I was immediately hired by a family-owned office supply company in Seattle as their sales manager. I worked for them for just over a year when the owner's son took over my position.

I was out of work for more than six months. Since we had spent every dollar we could to pay off our debts, we had no extra money to live on. Priscilla had a job waitressing, but it wasn't enough to sustain us. Everywhere I looked companies weren't hiring anyone with my qualifications.

This became a very difficult time of testing for me. There were times I would wake up in the middle of the night, go downstairs, and fall on my face crying out to the Lord in anguish because I couldn't provide for my family.

It got to the point that we couldn't pay our bills. I went to Pastor Bud seeking assistance from the church to pay our mortgage and an electric bill.

One day there was a knock on our door. When I opened the door, there was no one there but there sat a box full of food and an envelope containing some money. While these acts of love were a blessing to me and my family, it was one of the most humbling times of my Christian walk. I couldn't understand why the Lord was allowing me to go through this very difficult time.

During the next five years, the Lord used me in many various ministries as well as teaching me how to be His faithful servant. I wish I could say those years were only full of joy, but they did include many trials and situations that tested my faith. I am convinced the Lord always has a purpose for allowing us to experience trials in our lives as well as blessing. As painful as that period was, I am so grateful to God for that experience.

One day, Jim brought home a small garden snake he had found in the woods. We had an old fish tank so we said he could keep it in that. We had no idea what this would lead to. While Jim was in high school, he was hired by a local herpetologist who owned an exotic reptile pet store in Bellevue. Jim's snake collection grew from one snake to forty-two, two that were six feet long. All these snakes were kept in terrariums within his ten-foot-by-ten-foot bedroom. I think we as his parents have a special crown reserved for us in heaven for those years of living with his snakes!

In 1982, the Lord opened up an opportunity for me to become the manager of a department within World Concern called WorldCraft. World Concern is a Christian non-profit relief and development organization headquartered in Seattle, Washington. The purpose of WorldCraft was to assist in the development of cottage industries in third world countries. Our goal was to help impoverished people become self-sufficient by teaching them how to make products that could be sold in western countries.

That summer I was asked to go on a fact-finding tour throughout Asia. During this trip, I visited many of our current projects as well as looked for areas where we could expand. I visited eighteen cities in thirteen countries in five weeks.

My job was to take pictures and record specifics about each project. I made note of how many people were employed and how we could help them be more efficient in their production methods. I also recorded stories the workers told me about how the Lord has impacted their lives through World Concern.

The trip was long and exhausting and took its toll on me physically, mentally, and emotionally. One of my employees also accompanied me on this trip. Her responsibility was to help improve the products they were making to make them more attractive in western countries.

In Calcutta, India, we were met by a dedicated Christian social worker who drove us to the women's welfare house located in one of the worst slums in the area where Mother Teresa's charity has its hospital. Mostly young, unmarried, or divorced women and their children lived in a two-story building. As we drove up to the building, the smiling faces of about thirty young children greeted us. While there I took pictures of the girls making a variety of intricate lace products and learned some of their stories and how they have been rejected by their society. I gave each child and mother an individually wrapped butterscotch ball of candy. It was as if I had instantly become their friend, and they didn't want us to leave. My heart was filled with incredible joy to know that in this poverty-stricken place, God was using His people to help these women and children. To send us on our way, they sang several songs, and it was all I could do to keep from losing it emotionally.

While I was there to help and encourage the people I visited, God used them to encourage and strengthen my faith. During the months that followed, the Lord did many amazing things in the lives of our staff and in the lives of the people we were helping in the projects we were supporting.

In Kathmandu, Nepal, we visited a leather-making project run by men and women with leprosy. Going up some stairs to the flat roof of the building, I found three women preparing corn for their noonday meal, talking and laughing while two young girls and a boy were playing.

I showed the boy what he could see through the viewfinder of my telephoto lens, and he began talking, and laughing and encouraging the others to come and see. I couldn't understand what they were saying, and they couldn't understand me, but for an hour we had a very special time building a friendship. Finally, the oldest of the women was looking through the camera lens with her hands holding on to mine as I held the camera for her. I suddenly realized her hands were covered with leprosy sores, but it didn't matter. I had an amazing peace that God was in our midst.

In Hangzhou, China, the director of World Concern and I were on a handicraft fact-finding trip. We had been out walking and as we came back into our hotel, an American couple who were in China teaching English, approached us. We invited them to our room to chat. We discovered they were both Christians. One of them whispered, "We have to be careful what we say, because the rooms are most likely monitored." We enjoyed our visit with them greatly and left them with current magazines and the New Testament and Psalms I had carried with me throughout Asia. The Lord blessed us all by bringing us together, if only for a short time.

When World Concern decided to eliminate the WorldCraft ministry, I, too, was let go. This was again to be a time of great spiritual testing and learning. I wrestled with God, wondering why this had happened. Then one day as I was recounting to a friend all the successes this ministry had and lamenting why the Lord would just end it, he asked me, "Who was responsible for the success or failure of this ministry?"

"I was."

He then said, "No, you were not. Whose ministry was it? The Lord called you to be a part of His ministry, and He can do with it as He wishes. We must trust that He never does anything without having a divine and good purpose."

As we continued to talk, I realized that when the Lord calls me to a ministry, no matter how large or small, I am to do my very best for as long as I can. The outcome is up to the Lord.

Before I became a Christian, I believed my achievements were mine. Now, by the Lord's saving grace, I see all my achievements are a result of the Lord working in me and through me. What I do should always be for His honor and glory. I was learning to be grateful that He would choose me to be a part of what He is doing here on earth.

One Sunday morning during the summer after leaving World Concern, I was walking out of the church when I noticed a large overhead drawing of the church building and grounds on the bulletin board. Different sections of the grounds were numbered and members could sign up and take responsibility to maintain that section. There was a slightly raised section about four feet wide and forty feet long that ran between two parking areas. It had been bothering me for some time that no one had taken responsibility for cleaning the trash, rocks, overgrown ivy, and moss from that section. As I was looking at this drawing I became convicted that instead of complaining about it, I should do something about it, so I signed up to maintain that section.

A couple of weeks later, I drove to the church with my five-gallon bucket, clippers and trowel ready to do my thing. I had been working for a little more than an hour and was three quarters of the way finished. As I worked, I kept glancing around to see if anyone was watching me. I was hoping Pastor Bud or someone else would come by to see how hard I was working.

The dumpster was in the back of the church near the upper parking lot. I was coming up the hill to the parking lot with my full bucket when I saw the church chairman and his son walking down into the parking lot.

My bucket suddenly became much heavier and I ran my dirty hand across my face so brown sweat now rolled down my checks. We greeted each other and when he asked me what I was doing I told him how I had been cleaning up the overgrowth and trash between the two parking areas.

He then said, "God has given this piece of property to our church family here on Mercer Island. Isn't it a privilege to be led to maintain it for Him?" He said that he and his sons had been coming down and watering the lawns during the summer for over seven years. We talked for a few more minutes, then they went on their way to water the lawns.

I emptied my bucket then walked down to where I had been working. I didn't feel quite so proud of myself anymore. I dropped my bucket on the ground, knelt in the dirt, and pleaded with the Lord to forgive me. "Please forgive me for wanting to take credit myself for what You have called me to do for You. Why do I need to learn this lesson again?"

I then felt this warmth come over me that was different than the warmth of the hot sun. I can't explain it, but I knew then that the Lord was pleased with all the work I had done. From that point on, I didn't care if anyone came by or saw what I was doing, because I was now doing it to please God. The lesson He taught me that day has been a constant reminder of why I am here. It is not for my pleasure, even though I do receive pleasure from the things He has me do, but it for His good pleasure.

For a long time, I kept avoiding an issue I had not dealt with. It had to do with forgiveness. I knew my past actions had been forgiven by God as far as the east is from the west, however, I was not willing to forgive myself for the uncaring, unfeeling attitude I had when I did them. I had hurt many people, including my family. From time to time, the Holy Spirit would remind me that this was an unresolved issue between God and me, but still I avoided dealing with it.

Then, one day in 1990 as I was working in my home office, I was overcome with a conviction that I needed to deal with this sin and confess it to the Lord. I was so convicted that I fell to my knees weeping.

The problem all these twenty some years was not that the Lord had not forgiven me for the sin of my attitude; He had. It was that I was unwilling to forgive myself. When I finally did, it was as if a weight was lifted from my shoulders. Why it took me so long to deal with this sin is still not clear to me. I assume guilt had a big part in my denial.

TWENTY

The Blessing of the Lord

FROM 1983 TO 1993, THE Lord provided me with my own manufacturer's representative company. At times, I represented up to ten different manufacturers of medical supplies and equipment. My territory included the states of Washington, Oregon, and the upper half of Idaho. I also drove an average of thirty to forty thousand miles a year calling on medical supply companies, pharmacies, medical clinics, and hospitals.

I have done some dumb things in my life, but one of the dumbest is the time I had the brilliant idea of remodeling our kitchen.

Priscilla's older brother Bruce had for years been suffering with multiple sclerosis. To help her sister-in-law who was taking care of her husband, Priscilla flew back to Massachusetts to give Barbara a respite so she could take a trip with a friend.

Knowing this, I began to plot my surprise. My idea was to have our kitchen completely remodeled by the time she returned home. I planned to do this in the evenings and on the two weekends she was gone. I was so proud of myself for wanting to surprise Priscilla this way.

As soon as I dropped her off at the airport, I rushed home. I moved the dining room table against the couch in our ten-by-twenty-foot living and dining area, spread out a large plastic tarp on the floor, and began unloading all the contents of the cupboards and drawers and piling them on the plastic tarp. I also moved the refrigerator into the living room. This took longer than I had expected. I had no idea how much food and how many utensils we had stored in those drawers and cupboards.

My plan also included removing the electrical panel located in the kitchen and installing a new larger one. While I was at it, I thought I might as well remodel the small bathroom next to the kitchen.

I won't go into all the details; they are too painful to think about.

Our son Jim helped a little, but he really didn't want anything to do with this harebrained idea.

Ten days later, I picked Priscilla up from the airport. As we drove home, I did my best to explain my wonderful plan saying, "The problem, sweetheart, is that it has turned out to be a bigger job than I anticipated."

When she walked into our small condominium, she was greeted with the entire contents of our kitchen and bathroom on the living room and dining room floors. Priscilla was speechless. It took me another two weeks to finish the project. The women at church just stared at Priscilla in disbelief when she told them what she came home to. All the men said, "What on earth were you thinking?" Believe it or not, she still loves me.

In 1993, I dissolved my medical representative business because I was offered and accepted the position of western regional manager for AirSep Corporation. I worked for the domestic medical division overseeing a sales force responsible for the sales and distribution of oxygen and sleep apnea products in thirteen states. In addition, I was also responsible for a service and distribution center in Phoenix, Arizona, and a distribution center in Tukwila, Washington.

I went from driving thirty to forty thousand miles a year to flying over a hundred thousand miles a year. My travels took me as far north as Prudhoe Bay, Alaska and as far south as Hawaii. Priscilla had no desire to go with me to Prudhoe Bay, located just south of the North Pole, but was more than willing to accompany me when I traveled to Hawaii.

After five years, the company went through some financial restructuring which resulted in my being let go. This became another time of testing and seeking where the Lord was leading me.

Our marriage and my relationship with Jim and Jessica continued to flourish and grow. Priscilla and I found more and more opportunities to be involved with various ministry projects together.

This period of unemployment lasted about a year. Finally, with Priscilla's "encouragement," I went to Home Depot and filled out an application. I listed I had experience in lumber, electrical, gardening and hardware, but not much experience with plumbing. The next day I received a call and was hired. Where do you think they placed me, but in the plumbing department? Who says God doesn't have a sense of humor? I worked for Home Depot for about six months.

One day, I was told about a job opening for the position of church administrator at Mercer Island Covenant Church. After several interviews, I was hired. The first day on the job I showed up with my trusty Day-Timer expecting everyone to adhere to my very precise schedule and project expectations. Again, the Lord provided another learning opportunity for me. I'm grinning as I think about those early days in my new position. I learned to slow down and watch the Lord use me in ways He hadn't done in the past.

During this time, Jessica moved out of the house and began attending classes at the University of Washington.

For the next five and half years I grew even deeper spiritually despite some struggles and set-backs. After a year of working at the church, I felt a strong desire to be involved with full-time ministry. One day I stopped by the office of our pastor of children and families. During our conversation, I asked Pastor Steel what she was working on. She said she was taking a seminary class.

At that moment, I knew that this was what the Lord was directing me to do in preparation for full-time ministry.

After completing an in-depth application and interview process, I was accepted into a ministerial licensing program. Over the next three years, I took seven seminary classes enabling me to be a minister of the gospel with the Evangelical Covenant Church of America.

My main responsibility was pastor of administration. I was also called upon to do some counseling, conduct weddings, and preach during the transition between senior pastors.

Our family experienced two losses when Priscilla's mother and sister died within three months of each other. Priscilla's sister was the single parent of fourteen-year-old Christina. In January of 1996, we welcomed Christina into our home as her designated guardians, trusting God would work out the details. Our church and small group prayed us through many fears and challenges.

Christina's profound grief and deep hurt were compounded by her struggle with OCD. While we offered love, stability, and counseling, her full healing over the years had to come from the Lord. It is with amazement and praise to Him that we have seen her grow into a godly woman and ministering partner with her husband Scott.

Priscilla and I purchased a 900-square-foot cottage located on Lake Boren in 1996. My idea was to remodel and add onto this 1936 home. I discovered it was built in 1936 when I tore off the wallboard and found newspapers from 1936 stuffed inside for insulation.

The house was in worse shape than I originally thought. After many hours spent with the city planning commissioner, they allowed us to tear down the house and build the home that we currently live in.

This was a season of many changes for our family. Our daughter Jessica had met a nice young man, Chris, and they planned to be married. The wedding took place in May of 1997.

The week leading up to their marriage was a full one for me. I had been attending two long conferences in Las Vegas and wasn't able to get home until late that Wednesday night. Thursday and Friday were filled with running errands and helping with all the preparations. I had been told beforehand by several ladies that my responsibility was to do what I was told, pay the bills, and stay out of way, which I managed to do. I say that with a smile on my face because Jessica and Priscilla are super-organized people.

After the bridesmaids had walked down the aisle, the sanctuary doors were closed and Jessica and I stood there waiting to go in. Her hand grasped my arm and she said to me, "Dad, I love you." I started tearing up just as the doors opened to the sanctuary. Everyone rose as we slowly walked down the aisle.

As we stood in front of the pastor, Jessica's hand began to shake, so I put my hand on hers stroking it to comfort her. A twinge of pain ran through my heart when I realized I would not be the one to comfort her in the future; from now on it would be Chris. Priscilla and I are thrilled that Chris is the man Jessica had decided to marry.

In February of 2001, on a cold snowy morning, Hope, our first grandchild, was born to Chris and Jessica. I had the privilege of being in the delivery room while Jessica gave birth. It meant so much to me to pray for this newborn baby as I held her in my arms.

Then, in August of 2003, our grandson Aidan was born. Jessica wouldn't allow me in the room when Aidan was born, however. I guess she hadn't appreciated my humorous comments while she was in labor with Hope.

Hope is now sixteen and driving, and Aidan is fourteen. I have had many wonderful experiences with both of them. One of our favorite times together is the week each summer when our church puts on a day camp for about three hundred children. Hope and Aidan stay with us along with Wilson, their yellow lab. This has become our time to spoil them rotten.

They also love to spend hours in the lake and playing games with us in the evenings. As they have grown older, we enjoy celebrating their birthdays by sharing some event together rather than giving them a present. Priscilla and I just love spending time with them.

My dad died in February of 2005. It was a busy time for me between my work and helping Mom and my sister with all the preparations and then eventually sorting through all his things. I didn't really have time to mourn his death. I knew he was with the Lord and this brought great comfort to me.

About four months later, I was in the house by myself and happened to see a picture of my dad and me on the mantel of our fireplace. My grief finally came to the surface, and I dropped to my knees and cried. I couldn't have asked for a more loving and caring dad.

In December of 2006, my mom died. My mom was one of those people whom everyone loved. She probably said no more than a dozen negative or critical things in her entire life. This time I grieved right away.

Julie and I now needed to go through all the things that had been important to them and decide what to keep and what to give away. I had spoken to other people who struggled to do this, but I gained a new appreciation for what is involved in this sometimes-painful process. It felt as if we had lost both of them at the same time.

As I write this, I feel sad I can't share with them the many things that have happened in my life since the Lord took them home. I will see them again someday.

On July 1, 2007, at the age of sixty-two, once again I found myself out of work. A decision was made to change my position into two part-time positions. After a great deal of prayer and seeking advice from others, I resigned my position from the church we had been members of for thirty-one years. My faith seems to have matured because, as much as Priscilla and I love that church and especially the people in it, many who have become special friends, I felt complete peace about our leaving.

For several months prior to this, my son Jim and I had been planning a fishing trip. A couple of weeks after leaving my job, Jim and I took a nine-day fishing trip to Canada. Nine days on a boat sounds like a great trip to take if you are on a large cruise ship headed for some exotic destination. However, spending nine days with three men on a twenty-five-foot fishing boat is something you don't soon forget.

Other than spending an hour at a local resort to find a mechanic to do some repairs to our main engine, we didn't get off that boat for those nine days. I will say this trip tested my patience and endurance close to the edge. I think Jim went over the edge a couple of times, and yet it was a trip we will never forget. We caught five king salmon that ranged from forty-seven pounds to sixty-two pounds. Jim caught the sixty-two pounder that was the record size caught the year before.

Leaving our "fishing guide" behind, we took a float plane from Dawson's Landing in British Columbia to Renton, Washington. Priscilla met us at the plane and was stunned by the way we looked and smelled. I mean, what did she expect? We hadn't taken a bath or shaved in nine days. She refused to kiss me until I took a long hot shower and used a lot of soap.

I gave a lot of the salmon away, and we still had enough salmon for almost a year.

That fall I learned about a position at Newport Covenant Church for a pastor of congregational care. This was not a ministry I felt comfortable with, but I have always had the belief that when an opportunity arises, I should pursue it until the Lord closes that door. He didn't close the door, and in December of 2007, I was hired part-time in that position.

In March of 2008, I was offered the full-time position of director of ministry operations. In this position, I was placed in charge of the administrative and financial functions of the church as well as overseeing the church benevolence fund. I thought back to when I was out of work years before and needed help. If I hadn't experienced how the church helped us, I wouldn't have been able to relate as well to those who came to the church for financial help.

Truth be told, one of my most essential responsibilities was unplugging clogged toilets. The church has a pre-school of between 120 to 130 students, so this skill was put to frequent use. I grew to love the people at Newport and became involved in several different ministries there over the years.

Priscilla and I have been married forty-six years, and it has been the grace of our Lord that has healed and flourished our relationship. Where I have worked at over twenty different jobs over my lifetime, Priscilla is the steady consistent one in our family. In addition to a couple of waitressing jobs, Priscilla worked at her last position at Covenant Shores as their administrator for thirty years.

Priscilla and I retired from full-time work in September of 2012. Since then we have enjoyed a longer devotional time. Together, each morning we read a chapter from the Old and New Testaments in addition to reading a daily devotional. We also spend time praying for God's people, His church, our family, and whatever the Lord places on our hearts to bring before Him.

Since retiring, we have enjoyed going on many trips to other countries. I can't imagine living without her and the many things we do together. The Lord has done a wonderful thing in our lives and continues to do so even now.

The Lord has also blessed me with two wonderful, smart, and fun-loving children despite the very rough and troubled beginning I caused them many years ago.

Jessica has become a godly wife and mother who loves the Lord. Jim has gone from struggling with several of life's poor choices to becoming a man of God and being a part owner in Best Tree Service. Just thinking about what the Lord has done in their lives brings me great joy.

My life goes on as I do my best to serve the Lord wherever He directs my path. I continue to be involved with many church ministries and projects. They vary from fixing and building things as well as serving the church as the vice-chair of our elder board. I am also on the board of directors for an organization called CareNet of Puget Sound.

Over these past forty-plus years as a Christian, I had never before felt the Lord leading me to go on a mission trip even though there had been many opportunities to do so. One evening in the fall of 2014, our families and formation pastor expressed her desire to take a group of youth and adults to Rio Branco, Brazil during the next summer.

At the age of seventy, I was surprised by an overwhelming feeling that I was to go on this trip. It wasn't until we arrived in Rio Branco that the Lord revealed to me the reasons for my going. He gave me several opportunities to share my testimony, one being at their Sunday evening worship service in front of about three hundred people.

Despite some language barriers, we all fell in love with the people we had gone to serve. When it was time to leave, each of us felt we were leaving long-time friends.

When people hear my testimony, they sometimes marvel at what I have been through in my life and how far I have come in my walk with the Lord. I must confess, however, that these past forty years have not always been wonderful. I haven't always been obedient to God's Word.

I've had a couple of dry spells in my faith, and I haven't always lived my life in a way that has brought glory and honor to my Savior and Lord Jesus Christ. Yet, despite my failings and shortcomings, the Lord continues to use me and to touch the lives of others through me.

I spoke with a woman recently who has been a Christian since she was old enough to understand what following Jesus means. She mentioned how wonderful it would be to have a dramatic conversion and a testimony such as mine.

When I said "No, you don't," she seemed surprised. I told her, "From time to time, Satan throws my old self and ways back in my face and tries to tempt me with the pleasures I once thought were so exciting and fulfilling. Or he reminds me of the uncaring, hateful attitude I had toward the people I once cheated and hurt."

I shared with her how we were not different; we have all sinned. As Romans 3:22–24 says, "This righteousness from God comes through faith in Jesus Christ to all who believe. There is no difference, for all have sinned and fall short of the glory of God, and are justified freely by His grace through the redemption that came by Christ Jesus."

The Lord desires to use all of us who have become His disciples. All He requires of us is to be obedient and available to Him. It is the Holy Spirit who uses us to touch the lives of our "neighbors," those He brings across our path each day. It is the Holy Spirit of God who takes what we say and how we say it and makes it alive and powerful in the lives of others. It is the saving grace of our Lord Jesus Christ who, by His mercy, renews us each day as we place our trust and faith in Him.

After the apostle Paul's conversion on his way to Damascus, he was staying in the house of Ananias. When Paul had regained his sight, Ananias said: "The God of our fathers has chosen you to know His will and to see the Righteous One and to hear words from His mouth. You will be His witness to all men of what you have seen and heard" (Acts 22:14–15).

God's command to each of us is to be His witness to all those we come in contact with each day. It may only involve giving someone a cool drink of water or praying with them. What God asks of us is that we be ourselves. When He opens opportunities for us to share something about our life and faith, we are to respond, and the Holy Spirit will do the rest.

Every Christian has a powerful testimony because it is God who gives our testimony power. It is mind boggling to comprehend that the God who created the heavens and earth and everything in them and who holds everything together by His powerful hand, loves and cares about me and about you.

I was a rambunctious, happy-go-lucky California boy who grew up to fly helicopters in Vietnam. That experience changed me and my darker years contained alienation from my wife and family, my descent into the gambling lifestyle, and the loss of everything I owned. Despite myself, I didn't end up in prison or dead. Jesus found me and changed my life that night in church when I answered His call. He has given me the privilege of working for Him—truly a higher calling.

I leave you with this poem that has been a guide for my daily Christian life for many years:

Have You Earned Your Tomorrow?

Is anybody happier because you passed their way?
Does anyone remember that you spoke to them today?
The day is almost over and its toiling time is through;
Is there anyone to utter now a kindly word of you?
Can you say tonight in parting, with the day that's slipping fast,
That you helped a single person of the many that you passed?
Is a single heart rejoicing over what you did or said;

Does the person whose hopes were fading now with courage look ahead?
Did you waste the day, or lose it? Was it well or sorely spent?
Did you leave a trail of kindness or a scar of discontent?
As you close your eyes in slumber do you think that God will say,
"You have earned one more tomorrow by the work you did today?"
—Edgar Guest

I don't know what tomorrow will bring. The Lord may choose to use me for one more day or for twenty years or more. One thing is for certain, it is because of the Lord's love and grace that I am able to face each day and be used of Him to touch the lives of the others.

Order Information

CPSIA information can be obtained
at www.ICGtesting.com
Printed in the USA
BVHW041808081121
621080BV00014BA/622